HOUSE HACKER'S GUIDE TO THE GALAXY

Use Your Home to Make Millions & Retire Early

BRYCE STEWART

ISBN: 978-1-7363442-1-7

This book is dedicated to my wife Kelly.

No adventure is complete without a partner.

You're mine!

"Aut inveniam viam aut faciam."

"I shall either find a way or make one."

— Hannibal, 218 B.C.

When his generals told him crossing the Alps by elephant was impossible.

CONTENTS

INTRODUCTION

On July 18, 2008, I realized that I could not endure the career I had entered. I was leaving a meeting with my boss and felt like I had just been punched in the gut. Not only did I feel undercut but I felt like I'd just been swindled—not by my boss, but by the fact that I'd paid over $50,000 for a degree that "set me up" for a career like this.

Perhaps you're in a similar situation. You've taken all of the "recommended" steps in life:

+ studied hard for good grades in high school so you could get accepted into a reputable college.
+ narrowed down your desired major and completed all the coursework required to get a degree.
+ polished your resume leading up to graduation so you could find a decent employer and begin paying back your school debt.

Yet despite all this, you realized after two and a half years that your job is much less fun than college was, but it's going to take twenty years of working a not-fun job in order to pay off four years of schooling.

And as you scroll through Facebook, you wonder how anyone can afford to have a house, a nice car, vacations, a spouse, kids, and free time.

Seeing this, you become depressed when you begin doing Financial Math and discover that you aren't building any wealth and that in order to survive and have a family who can eat dinner, you're going to need to spend forty-five years in a cubicle, office, or desk.

You decide to drink alcohol or some other "escape activity" to take your mind off of this cruel setup.

While that was my life at one point, I'm now under forty years old, and I've been retired for five years. I am unemployed and I have no salary. Yet my net worth is over $1 million, my financial position is fairly comfortable, and I earn more than enough money each month to meet the needs of my family.

I wrote this book because thousands of people have asked me how they can achieve the same result through local real estate. I can't give you a guarantee that your results will match mine exactly, (you'll discover that I caught some lucky breaks and had access to unique help) but my journey demonstrates what can be done. After all - I had my fair share of obstacles and difficulties which might be absent in your journey.

THE PROBLEM WITH A JOB—
AND WHY I WALKED AWAY

In July of 2008, I was a sixth-grade teacher working at a middle school in Bethlehem, Pennsylvania. My third year of teaching started in a few short weeks. The building principal had called me up in the middle of the summer and asked me to meet in her office. That's right; I got called to the principal's office—it feels just as ominous to a teacher as it does to a student!

In fairness, I don't think my principal realized the magnitude of the gut-punch she delivered. She wasn't rude, mean-spirited, or vindictive. In fact, I liked and admired her. But this didn't diminish my crisis.

A bit of context: every year, public school teachers around the country are formally evaluated by the principal in their building. A teacher's continued employment and certification depend upon obtaining at least a sufficient score from their administrator. Since teachers operate semi-autonomously within their classrooms, the evaluation typically takes the form of a planned observation of a lesson by the principal. In my previous years, that meant my principal visited a few times and watched me teach my students while she scribbled notes on a clipboard.

But during the prior school year (2007–2008), Pennsylvania and the Bethlehem Area School District began a new approach to evaluations. Instead of the normal, principal-wielding-a-clipboard-during-a-lesson observations, sixth-grade teachers created a "self-directed" project during the school year that supported their curriculum or classroom in some way and presented it to the principal in late spring. The requirements weren't specific, and teachers had a great deal of choice in what they could create. If their self-directed project was good, teachers could receive a satisfactory or even superior score on their evaluation.

I can distinctly remember many of my peers creating projects that were simply designed to "check the box" for the principal's evaluation. One teacher created a "homework page" link on their website so kids and parents could check it at home (this probably took a half hour to create, total).

But I took the project a little more seriously. I wanted to create something that would truly benefit me and the students I was teaching. On top of that, during the 2007–2008 school year, my wife, Kelly, and I found out we were expecting our first child. I assumed that my 2008–2009 school year would include late nights with a newborn, as well as an exhausted wife. Thus, I wanted to create a self-directed project that would save me time and effort in the upcoming year.

So I set to work creating a truly monumental project: I would plan out every single activity, lesson, daily procedure, assignment, and resource in my upcoming year—all 180 days! I taught social studies, and our curriculum was less than robust. My students were confused and bored by the worksheets provided by the textbook publisher. So every day after school, I created my own versions which covered the same material. The publisher had insufficient videos and ancillary activities, so I researched, downloaded, and categorized videos for every single topic we studied. I created videos of my own, and activities to support them. I created tests and quizzes, compiled primary resource materials, and much more.

On top of that, I created a master 180-page keynote presentation (one page for each school day) with a list of daily objectives, procedures, state standards, and hyperlinks to relevant videos, assignments, and evaluations. Because I knew I would have a young daughter in the upcoming year, I created a resource that would allow me to simply press "play" at the beginning of the year and then reap the rewards of my hard work. I must have spent over a hundred hours (on top of my normal teaching hours!) creating my project.

Each afternoon, when all the other teachers had gone home, I stayed in my classroom working. Kelly would call and ask, "When are you coming home?"

"As soon as I can, dear. Remember, we'll both benefit from my hard work next year when I can leave each day at 3:30."

In late spring, I proudly brought my materials to the project evaluation meeting with my principal. I believed that she would be impressed with the volume of work I had done. I also planned to share this resource with my fellow sixth-grade social studies colleagues, and I figured that would score "team-player" points. But my principal must have been distracted that day—I don't think she grasped the amount of work I'd done or that I had created a highly detailed curriculum all on my own. I left the meeting with a satisfactory evaluation score and a bruised ego.

My consolation, of course, was that I still had an incredible resource that was going to save me loads of time in the upcoming year—or so I thought. The school year ended uneventfully, my wife and I vacationed for a week and enjoyed our last summer together as a child-free couple, and I had high hopes for the upcoming school year—until that fateful meeting in my principal's office on July 18th.

I went in and sat down in front of her desk. We exchanged pleasantries and she eventually got around to the reason for our meeting: she needed to juggle different staff into different positions, and she wanted to move me from teaching social studies to teaching science.

Stunned silence.

"Ummm, do you remember the self-directed project I showed you this year?" I asked.

"Refresh my memory," she responded.

"I basically rewrote and extended the entire social studies curriculum. I made interactive lesson plans for the entire year, and—"

"Don't worry, I will provide you with the science curriculum. I can even get you an extra key to the building if you need to come in during the next few weeks and start prepping experiments and materials and stuff."

Poof! In an instant, my hundred hours of work evaporated. I left her office, bewildered and upset. Twenty days later, Kelly gave birth prematurely to our daughter. We brought her home after a brief stay at the hospital, and I started trying to adjust to fatherhood. But I had to leave Kelly and little baby Laney every day, go to my classroom, and scramble to learn a brand new curriculum and subject before the school year started.

Effectively, my hourly wage had been cut in half: I was earning the same salary but needed to put in more hours to do all the additional work. After school every day during that next year, I still had to stay late every afternoon to learn the new curriculum and to prepare and clean up experiments. I felt like my previous year's self-directed project, and all the accompanying efficiencies, had been stolen from me.

That was the year I decided in my heart that I refused to have my economic life and compensation dictated by someone else. I began to desire an economic escape plan. But what could I do? I needed this job. So did my family. There was no way I could go back to college, get another degree, and start my career all over again. I suspected the High Income Train left the station without me when my nineteen-year-old self chose elementary education as my college major. If I'd wanted to amass enough wealth to walk away from an unpleasant job situation, I should have gotten a degree in finance, law, or medicine or perhaps created the next Facebook or Microsoft in my dorm room. Surely, it was too late now . . .

* * *

Seven years later, in August of 2015, at age thirty-five, I walked into my principal's office. This time, I had called the meeting. After exchanging pleasantries, my principal shared plans for how the staff would be "raising the bar" in the upcoming year and how we all had to "elevate our game." I listened politely until there was a pause. Then I said, "Well . . . I wish you the best of luck, but it's going to be without me. I just submitted my resignation to the HR department downtown. It's been great—I'm retiring." We shook hands, I walked out the door, and I went home to spend time with Kelly and my (now) four daughters.

This retirement was possible because the passive income I was earning from owning local real estate fully funded my family's budget. I no longer needed a job. Having my time and efforts squandered by a less-than-receptive boss taught me an important lesson: No one else is planning my economic future. No one cares about my time the way I do. No one will increase my compensation unless I do it myself. So I did it myself—with a good deal of help along the way.

Perhaps you are in a similar situation and have a similar desire. Maybe you've suffered similar indignities in your line of work. I've personally coached enough dissatisfied employees to realize that teachers don't have an exclusive claim to unjust working conditions or squandered efficiencies. Like me, you might have worked really hard to build something meaningful, hoping it would free up your future time or increase your future compensation, only to have it taken away from you on a whim.

In the pages ahead, I'll share how buying and managing local real estate earned me financial freedom. I will provide a road map for those who want to achieve the same, sharing the lessons I learned along the way.

———

To get the most out of this book, and to begin creating a blueprint
for *your own financial freedom*, download my free workbook PDF at
brycestewart.net/househacker

2

THE FINANCIAL SHIP IS SINKING

The squandering of a hundred hours invested in my self-directed project was just the tip of the crisis iceberg. It got worse. By 2008, Kelly and I were in bad shape on many fronts—and "early retirement" was not even in our vocabularies.

We had married in 2006, and in the months leading up to our wedding, Kelly lived with her parents in Bethlehem, about an hour north of West Chester, PA—where I was living with my folks. I had worked a few jobs during the three years since attending Grove City College, but I hadn't managed to land one that would provide enough monthly income to live in my own apartment and pay for my car loan and my school loan. So I still lived with my parents, in my high school bedroom.

During our six-month engagement, I worked in the educational world's equivalent of Purgatory known as long-term substitute teaching. My then-fiancé Kelly was working an administrative job in Bethlehem. While looking for a place of our own for after the wedding, an opportunity arose in Bethlehem to purchase a new, luxury, one-bedroom condominium for what seemed like a good price (if this were a movie, I would add ominous music here since it ended up being very UNaffordable). In all fairness, it was in a truly incredible condo complex. A local developer had purchased an old Bethlehem Steel foundry building right next to the Lehigh River and converted it into 172 condominium units. It's still a very nice and unique place to live—but it ended up costing us dearly and threatening our financial solvency.

At the time, the housing market and economy, in general, had experienced four–five years of incredible growth. Home values climbed month after month, year after year. You simply couldn't lose buying real estate, whether you were a homeowner or an investor. Plus, we got an early deal on a sales contract and would be buying for less than what comparable units were selling for.

So in May of 2006, we closed on the condo two weeks before our wedding, using what is known as a 5/1 adjustable rate mortgage—a loan product that has a fixed interest rate for the first five years but can vary widely thereafter (more ominous music; these loans ended up sinking a lot of borrowers in the 2007–2008 financial crisis). After our honeymoon, we moved into our new place and started our life together.

I landed a permanent teaching job in the fall, a position I kept for the next nine years. Despite the self-directed project fiasco and the other drawbacks that eventually encouraged me to retire early, I must confess that this job was a huge blessing, all things considered. And it was crucially necessary during this step in our financial journey.

With two low but reasonable salaries, we "tightened our belts" and managed to pay off my car loan and college loan in a year and a half. In retrospect, this probably saved us from bankruptcy later.

By 2008, the Great Recession was in full swing. The economic "sky" was falling, banks were failing, homeowners and investors were foreclosing on homes, property values were plummeting, and Kelly was pregnant. We realized that our one-bedroom condominium probably wouldn't be ideal for a family of three, so we started looking at options for moving elsewhere.

Two horrific realities became evident right away. First, we could not sell our one-bedroom condominium for anywhere close to our outstanding principal balance. (We owed close to $150,000, and similar units were now only selling for $85,000.)

The second horrific realization was that we could not charge enough rent to cover our fixed costs of ownership! I'm embarrassed to admit it—but prior to this, we simply had not done the math on what our condo was costing us each month. I had focused most of my attention on automobile and college debt elimination. I wrongly viewed the mortgage payment, Home Owner's Association (HOA) dues, and property taxes as personal monthly bills—just like electricity, water, and cable. In reality, we were financially responsible for the $1,400 total fixed costs even after moving. Since similar condo units were renting for around $1,050, we could expect to lose around $350 each month, even with a tenant paying us rent! Initially, I leaned toward hiring a Realtor to handle renting out the condo, but Realtors generally charge one full month's rent as a commission, which would only compound our losses.

"We can do it ourselves," Kelly suggested. "My landlords in college didn't use Realtors. They had a pretty simple-looking lease that was probably just a Word document. There are lots of Google hits for 'blank Pennsylvania lease.' Let's just use a boilerplate version from the internet." I agreed.

Confident that we could draw up our own lease, we created a rental ad on Craigslist and priced our condo at $1,095. An adjunct professor at Lehigh University in Bethlehem came to view it and agreed to rent. But even this best-case-scenario meant we would lose $305 every month, at the very time when our family size (and costs!) were expanding. We also did not know how many hours Kelly could continue to work after having the baby. At the time, my bi-weekly paychecks were $1,119 and my wife's were $950, for a total monthly take-home pay of $4,138. Before having the baby and moving out of the condo, our monthly financial picture looked like this:

+	$2,238	my monthly take-home pay
+	$1,900	Kelly's monthly take-home pay
-	$1,400	fixed monthly housing costs
	$2,738	monthly budget

Before getting pregnant, this monthly budget had been sufficient to meet the needs of two young adults. It allowed us the occasional date night, gym memberships, groceries, utilities, automobile insurance, gas and maintenance, savings for vacations and Christmas, and everything else. For the next decade, this ~$2,700 would be the functional baseline amount I used to gauge whether we were getting ahead or falling behind financially. But with a monthly rental loss and a new child, that budget was going to be severely squeezed.

As the 2007–08 school year drew to a close, we signed a lease with the adjunct professor starting August 1. I worked a temp job all summer and Kelly, eight months pregnant, spent her lunch hours and late afternoons searching all over our city to try to find a two-bedroom apartment that felt clean and safe enough to bring a newborn baby home to. It nearly brings me to tears when I look back and realize it was the closest thing to nesting that she could manage, given our circumstances. I can recall one particular conversation that I'm not proud of:

"Bryce, I looked at three different two-bedroom apartments today for $950 each, and they were all somewhere I wouldn't want to live," my wife told me.

"That's because your standards are too high, Kelly. We are in dire straits! We will be losing money every month! We simply can't afford to shop for a 'princess's apartment.'"

"Okay," Kelly frowned. "Why don't you sit and look at the available apartments listed on Craigslist with me?"

We sat together and found a two-bedroom, one-bathroom apartment listed for $750 per month. There were no pictures, only a description. We called the listed phone number and spoke to the landlord, who scheduled a showing with us.

"There," I said. "That wasn't hard." We showed up at our scheduled appointment two days later. The landlord let us in and walked us up to an apartment that reeked of smoke, pet dander, and worse. The refrigerator was in the bathroom. The potential baby room was in a hot, third-floor bedroom that was a barely-converted attic. We politely finished touring and then said, "We'll let you know."

When we got out to the car and shut the doors, Kelly burst into tears. I almost did too. While $750 was very affordable, it apparently meant living in a craphole apartment. I emotionally resigned myself to paying over $1,200 a month for a two-bedroom apartment in one of the bigger complexes in town, telling myself (lying, really) we would figure out how to make the numbers work. That was the same summer and same week that my principal called me into her office and switched me from teaching social studies to science. It was a hard week.

Reluctantly, we scheduled a showing at one of the big apartment complexes in Bethlehem and walked through the cookie-cutter apartment with the management company's desk agent. It was $1,200 a month but adequate and clean. We filled out an application and left.

Thank God for Kelly's tenacity. The very next day, she kept looking online for apartments and called me breathlessly during my lunch.

"I found a place that looks awesome!!" she yelled.

"How much is it?"

"$850! And the pictures show nice hardwood floors, a clean bathroom and kitchen, and even a dining room! It's also right downtown, two blocks from my work!"

We booked a showing with the landlord that very night. Although it was a third-floor walk-up apartment, the pictures hadn't lied. It was nice, clean, and neat. After looking all through the apartment, I approached the landlord.

"You said the rent is $850?"

"Yes."

"Is there any way you could do $825? We're expecting our first child and money is tight. We can definitely afford the rent, but we're counting every dollar."

"I think we could do that."

HOORAY!!! We practically danced down the steps. The next day, we showed up to her office early, with $825 for rent and $825 for security deposit in hand. We signed the lease, took the keys, and thanked her profusely. She even agreed to let us begin moving stuff in before August 1, when our lease started. To make things even better, the apartment was two blocks from Kelly's office, and she had negotiated with her boss to allow her to keep twenty of her weekly work hours plus weekend events after the baby arrived.

The difference in rent between this $825 downtown gem and the $1,200 cookie-cutter apartment in the big complex was $375 per month (one-third of my bi-weekly take-home pay). More importantly, we were dropping our housing costs from $1,400 per month while living in our condo to $825 in the new apartment—a whopping $575 difference.

But we would simultaneously be losing $305 per month from the cash-hemorrhaging condo, so our budget really only improved $270. And Kelly's $950 every two weeks was dropping to $525 because of reduced hours. I notched a $50 per paycheck raise that school year, giving us the following monthly scenario:

+	$2,338	my monthly take-home pay (with +$100 monthly raise)
+	$1,050	Kelly's new monthly take-home pay
-	$305	loss on condo carrying costs.
-	$825	rent at gem apartment
	$2,258	monthly budget

This diminished budget hurt, but it was at least manageable. The new baby meant we would probably be spending less money eating at restaurants and traveling to see friends. And although the move from luxury condo to third-floor apartment was a huge discount in monthly housing costs, it really didn't diminish our standard of living very much. Yes, the bathroom was dated. No, the kitchen didn't have granite like our condo. But it was clean, we had a room for the baby, and we were happy!

It was a big win for my psyche too. After having my self-directed project efficiencies taken from me at work, this financial victory gave me hope for our future.

Twelve days after moving in, Kelly gave birth to our first daughter, Laney—premature, but perfectly healthy. I tackled the new school year with refreshed energy, and we began saving all of the extra cash we could. Things felt like they were finally starting to turn.

Then one day, about five months into the school year, I came home after work and walked up the steps to our apartment. I opened the door and found Laney crying in a crib and Kelly lying in the middle of the living room, bawling her eyes out.

"Are you hurt? What's wrong?" I practically shouted.

"I'm pregnant AGAIN!" she cried.

Cue the ominous music . . .

LESSON 1:
EVEN IF IT'S NOT IDEAL, GET A JOB!

This first phase of our investing journey taught us some very important lessons crucial for any aspiring real estate investor. The very first lesson should be obvious: both my job and my wife's job were absolute blessings.

Some people encourage aspiring investors NOT to get a normal job because you need to be "all-in" on your dream, or you need to learn to analyze and acquire real estate deals exclusively using "other people's money." While I'm a fan of both of those ideas, you should be pursuing them in your spare time. Prime time is for making a salary and getting a guaranteed income. If you need extra space in your calendar or your brain, cancel Netflix and stop going out to bars on Friday and Saturday nights.

A "normal" job will be a blessing for you, just as ours were. Since my job was at a higher salary than I had ever earned, this salary eventually would be the basis of getting approved for several mortgages during my investing career. So the value of that job is hard to overstate. It also meant that we could eat, put gas in our cars, and heat our home. These things are all (obviously) necessary for an aspiring investor. Having two salaries, with no kids, allowed us to begin on a decent financial footing.

A second, HUGE benefit of my job was that my wife and I both got terrific health insurance benefits through my school district. Eventually, we had each of our four daughters while I was still employed as a teacher. Because of various complications, all four of my daughters were born through Caesarean section procedures. The hospital sent us a copy of the total bill for each birth, and the average cost was $30,000. But because teachers' health insurance plans are generally top-notch, the pregnancies and deliveries were treated as single "conditions." Thus, we were only responsible for the co-pay portion of the initial pregnancy OB/GYN appointment, a whopping $10 per child. There is no way we could have reached financial freedom if we had needed to shoulder the financial burden of those healthcare costs.

Yet another benefit was my summer break. After teaching for a decade, I believe no teacher could possibly remain in the profession without the summer break. It is necessary to emotionally recover and to prepare for the upcoming school year. For ambitious investors like myself, however, this two-and-a-half-month hiatus provided an opportunity to work a second job, pursue master's degree credits, and eventually get my real estate license. I'm also not sure if I would have had the energy or time to keep hitting the pavement until we found that $825 two-bedroom apartment if I'd been working a serious (non-temp) job at the time. This extra time in the summer was crucial to my success year after year, and I'm thankful I had a job which allowed it. Although it doesn't need to be teaching, pursue a job that gives you some type of flexibility to begin organizing your financial house and building your empire.

A teaching job was not the main goal of my financial journey. But it was necessary in Phase 1. A job gave me stability, credibility, and a valuable network. And a job can get you a mortgage, which will come in very handy in acquiring real estate. Get a job.

LESSON 2:
EXTRA MONEY IS FOR KILLING DEBT

The second lesson learned in Phase 1 of our story is something I only really mentioned in passing. We made it a priority to pay down debt during that first year and a half, even while we were "living large" in the luxury one-bedroom condo. We earned staggered, bi-weekly paychecks, and I can remember using almost all of my wife's $950 direct deposit paychecks to pay down some of her consumer debt, then my car loan, and then eventually my school loan. It sounds like I was stealing her money to pay my debts, but all our money went into the same bank account, so it may as well have been my $950 every other week. Besides, I used my paychecks to pay all of the bills and keep us housed. We actually had a couple of fights about it, because on a few occasions my wife had consumptive plans for that money and was upset when she realized it was already gone.

But if we hadn't paid those loans off before the first baby arrived, we would have been sunk when things got tough. The $480 drop in our monthly lifestyle budget after renting the gem was difficult enough! Can you imagine still having car and school loans AND landing in the $1,200 apartment AND (for some folks) credit card debt? Brutal! I should mention that my wife had no college or car debt when we got married. If she had, there is simply no way we would have survived financially.

If you are reading this while still in high school, pay attention: if you can help it, don't take a loan for a car, ever. It's a huge stumbling block and will get in the way of your financial freedom. As I write this, I'm financially free and a millionaire. Yet I drive a fourteen-year-old Honda CR-V, which I've never had a loan on. It's the best machine I've ever owned, and it barely takes any money out of my pocket each month, which is the highest praise an automobile can achieve. Cars steal your money. Your relationship with them is solely about mitigating loss until they cost as much to you as a stick of gum costs now. More on this topic later.

If you're reading this while still in high school, pay even more attention here: your number one priority should be to get a college degree with either no debt or the least amount of debt possible. If this seems impossible, you should at least calculate very carefully what kind of income you can expect from the degree you are seeking to determine how quickly your income can eliminate the debt you will accrue. The world needs elementary school teachers, social workers, and artists—but the world will not pay these people enough to eliminate the $100,000 debt that often accompanies the degree. Don't assume that what you are "passionate" about as an eighteen-year-old will still hold your passion when it takes twenty years of hard labor to pay it off. Or hold off on your passion until after becoming financially free, when you can pursue and enjoy your passion without the pressure of it needing to financially support you.

To graduate with the least amount of debt possible, you can work for a year, save money, and experience what the real world is like. Then go to college with some funds to pay for it. Or go to trade school—which results in decent wages with very little debt, as well as a skill set that will be extremely helpful for future real estate investing. Or do two years at community college and then transfer to a four-year college to finish up. I promise you're not missing anything worthwhile by skipping the typical four-year experience at a big-name college. And on that note, opt to go to a cheaper college.

I went to a small-name college. I remember being embarrassed during my senior year of high school because all my peers were applying to and getting accepted at big-name colleges, while I had committed to a school no one ever heard of. I was half-tempted to withdraw and apply to the University of Big Football and Parties, or Well-Known-Overpriced-Liberal-Arts-College, like everyone else. I'm so glad I didn't. Please hear me: no one cares. Once you graduate, no one cares! Half the kids who go to these prestigious colleges drop out without a degree. Much of the remaining half struggles with their debt for decades.

I lucked out by going to a great college that is consistently ranked as one of the best deals in colleges and universities, so my debt was not insurmountable. If either my wife or I had brought significant college debt to the marriage, it would have destroyed our chances at financial freedom and early retirement—and that is something worthwhile.

If you've already graduated college and are carrying school debt, kill it! Get rid of car debt first, but then kill the school loans! Until those loans are gone, every drink, every restaurant, every vacation is just you spending away your chance at financial freedom. Wait tables at night. Get a side hustle. Whatever it takes, kill that debt!

LESSON 3:
BUY HOUSES THAT RENT FOR MORE THAN THEIR CARRYING COSTS

In Phase 1 of our story, we made a stupid mistake of buying a first home (our one-bedroom condo) that had carrying costs higher than what the home could rent for. We should have done the math before ever signing our agreement of sale, but we didn't know any better. Achieving financial freedom through real estate is all about buying houses that generate rents higher than your carrying costs so with each additional house you buy, you increase your monthly income. Our very first step was in the wrong direction, and as of the writing of this book, I still own that same condo and have lost money on it every month for thirteen years.

Imagine if we'd owned a cheaper condo, co-op, or small ranch home when our first baby arrived and we needed to move. In 2006, we could have easily secured something with carrying costs of $850 that could have rented for $950. Then, when we needed to move, we would have been earning $100 per month, instead of losing $305. That variance of $405 would have been huge for a teacher and his family!

So make sure you do the math and ensure average rent for your home will be higher than your carrying costs. Generally, this is your PITI number, or principal & interest, taxes, insurance (homeowner's). These are the costs you will have to continue paying for as long as you own the home. Normally, a tenant will pay the monthly cost for utilities like electricity, gas, water, and trash. So your profit (or lack of profit) will be the total monthly rent minus the PITI. If you own a condo like we did, make sure to include HOA dues too.

LESSON 4:
DON'T FALL FOR THE MIDDLE-CLASS TRAP OF GETTING YOUR DREAM HOUSE AND CAR RIGHT AWAY

Many of my peers began looking for their "dream house" as soon as they found out they were pregnant with their first child. The thinking goes something like this:

"We're having kids now. It's time to buy the typical four-bedroom, two-and-a-half bathroom center hall Colonial-style house offered by American Suburbia. With both of our salaries, we can get approved for a mortgage on a place like this. We will also be needing a large SUV to safely carry around the new baby, in case it snows three feet one night and we have to drive somewhere before the roads are plowed."

I know plenty of seemingly intelligent married couples, both with college degrees, who fell for this financial trap. Obviously, if you get a thirty-year mortgage based on two salaries, both of you will have to continue working for the next thirty years in order to afford it. And since both of you will be forced to continue working, you will have to budget for daycare/summer care for your children. And that "necessary" SUV will have a higher loan payment, insurance payment, and fuel costs than a more reasonable used car. These items comprise the middle-class trap, and they are the enemy of financial freedom.

Later, I will detail what purchase would have been optimal when we first got married (it was our second purchase), and what I believe is a great option for anyone in our situation. In the meantime, if you already own a condo, co-op, or home, begin evaluating it to determine its rentability. Find out what similar properties are renting for so you can determine how much you would make/lose monthly if things in your life went sideways and you needed to live elsewhere but couldn't sell the place.

LESSON 5:
SMART RENTING COUNTS AS REAL ESTATE INVESTING

It would be tempting to think that my wife and I had only experienced real estate investing failure up to 2008, or perhaps that we hadn't even begun investing in real estate yet. That's not true.

I had breakfast with a young twenty-one-year-old a few months ago who was renting a room at his mom's house and told me that he "really wants to get into real estate investing." He was extremely surprised when I told him that he is already investing in real estate. Anyone who is paying to live somewhere is investing in real estate because somewhere within their living arrangement is an opportunity to optimize their financial condition.

When my wife persistently kept looking for an affordable, decent place to rent, she was investing in real estate. Her persistence saved us $350 in cash flow per month (my negotiating with the landlord saved us the other $25). We could have easily settled on the $1,200 cookie-cutter apartment, and been forced to pay the extra $375 every month.

I know plenty of investors who would happily purchase a home or apartment that generates $300 per month in profits, so $375 is not an insignificant sum even for investors. But if you had offered my pregnant wife and me the choice between such an investment OR renting the gem apartment, the gem still would have been a better choice because it altered our cash flow in a more positive way during a needy period of life.

Perhaps you've told yourself you want to invest in real estate later in your life or that you're ready now but can't find deals. Nonsense. Start with your abode—I guarantee you can financially optimize your living scenario. Two years ago, we paid $7,500 for a new, high-efficiency gas boiler in our home (we own a house now). It cut our yearly heating bill by $2,300, giving us a 31 percent annual return on investment (ROI). It also delivers more comfortable and balanced heat in our home. I consider it a superior real estate investment, and it didn't even include acquiring additional property and the accompanying responsibilities. It simply lowered our costs and keeps more money in our pockets each year. These small steps are steps toward financial freedom, and they force your brain to start thinking like a real estate investor.

A GLIMMER OF HOPE

"Pregnant AGAIN?" How could this happen?" I said as if Kelly was solely responsible.

"I don't know, I don't know, I don't know! There's no way I'm going to be able to keep working."

That had been my first thought, too. After all the time we spent arranging our financial life and optimizing our living conditions, I'd failed to consider what would happen if/when we had another kid. We were happy to be expecting another child, but my mind was already hurtling into money panic mode.

It simply wouldn't work, financially speaking. We were already losing $480 each month, relative to our monthly lifestyle budget of a year earlier. Now Kelly was almost certainly going to need to quit her job, which meant we'd be short another $1,050 each month. And now we would have two babies who would need diapers, clothing, food, and more.

I cried. I'm serious. I was certain this was the financial "kiss of death." That night, I took a walk by myself to be alone with my thoughts. This is why people wait to get married. This is why people wait to have kids. This is why people get a degree in finance, law, or medicine instead of a degree in elementary education. I've screwed up Big Time and my kids are going to grow up in poverty. We'll never have a house, we'll never be able to afford our food— let alone anything nice. No vacations, no activities, clunker cars forever.

I tried to think through financial survival options. It was late January, and I had about nine months to figure something out before the baby arrived. We still had a little bit of money saved from my temp job the previous summer, and I'd probably have to work another temp job in the upcoming summer. But how long can I keep that up? Even that break-neck, twelve-month work schedule will only keep us solvent while we stay in this $825 gem apartment. Two kids will very quickly need more space. And the only reason I've been willing to work a temp job during the summer months (when I should be emotionally recuperating) is to try to go GET AHEAD financially—not just stay in one place!

As I walked, I started contemplating an old idea from five years in my past. The very first job I worked after college wasn't in education. From 2003–2004, I had worked for a title insurance and settlement company in West Chester, PA. These are the companies that conduct real estate purchase and refinance transactions and disburse money to the buyers, sellers, and banks at closing. I had worked there in several roles, none of which had really turned into anything that could become a career (which is why I went into long-term substitute teaching).

While taking my walk, one memory that stuck out was a conversation with a coworker of mine at the title company. He and I had both been twenty-three years old, and while we were getting to know each other, he asked me where I lived.

"Uhh . . . I still live with my folks, in my high school bedroom. My dad says I need to pay him $300 a month because I eat a lot of food and I'm a college graduate now," I admitted sheepishly. "How about you?"

"I live in Norristown (a smaller city west of Philadelphia). My college roommate and I bought a four-unit apartment building. Each apartment has two bedrooms. We live in one of the units, and we rent the other three out to tenants."

I was immediately skeptical. I was pretty certain only big companies owned apartments, not twenty-three-year-olds. "What do you mean, you bought it? You two guys own it yourselves?"

"Yes."

"Wait . . . isn't it expensive? Isn't there a high mortgage? How can you afford something like that?"

"Well, the mortgage payment isn't exactly low. But we use the rents from the other three units to pay it every month."

"Okay. But aren't the property taxes high?"

"They aren't too bad. But we pay those with the rents too. And we pay the homeowner's insurance the same way."

My face was probably looking increasingly dumbfounded. "But I bet there's a high water bill, right? And the electric and cable bills must be insane." I figured he and his roommate were probably using their salaries to fund all the extra costs associated with their little "experiment."

"Well, I couldn't tell you about our tenants' water and electric bills—they each have their own meters, so that's between them and the utility companies. But to be honest, we pay our utility bills with the rents from the other three units, too."

Now I was visibly stupefied. "You mean you're living there for free? I'm paying $300 a month for my stinking high school bedroom!!!!"

"That's not all," he said. "It also puts $100 a month in each of our pockets."

My knees almost buckled and my head started spinning. I was . . . angry. Why hadn't anyone told me this could be done? I got good grades throughout my school years. I had two well-educated parents with master's degrees. I graduated cum laude from a highly selective college. But no one had ever told me you could make money from something besides a job.

"How . . . who . . . told you to do this?" I asked. "How did you figure out how to do it?"

"I read a book called Rich Dad, Poor Dad. I'll bring you my copy tomorrow. Listen, I need to get back to my desk and get to work."

"One more thing," I stammered. "If you're living for free, what do you do with the money you get from this job?"

"I pay back my parents," he admitted. "We borrowed the down payment from them. In six more months, they will be fully reimbursed. Then I'll probably start saving up for another down payment."

He brought the book to work the next day, and I devoured it in a day and a half. The seed was planted. I vowed that if I ever got the chance to do something like that, I would take it.

Five years later, this entire episode replayed in my head as I was taking a walk in late January of 2009 and wondering how to provide for two kids and a wife. I had been really impressed by that coworker, and I had wanted to do something similar. The problem was, no one had ever walked up and offered me a four-unit apartment building, so I had no opportunity to copy him.

But if anyone ever needed to live for free, it was my pregnant wife, my infant daughter, and me. So I resolved to begin investigating and see if anything came of it. I finally turned the corner on the street to our apartment, and I walked home to find a sleeping mama and a sleeping baby girl. I slept too.

"Are you kidding?" Kelly screeched when I told her my idea the next morning. "How on earth do you think we can buy another house? We're already losing money on a condo every month, and you want to buy more? We can barely eat—how do you think we'll save up enough for a down payment?"

I love my wife, and she's been very supportive over the years. But this wasn't one of those moments.

"Well, we can't stay here forever!" I yelled back. "I'm just trying to get us somewhere that will put us ahead." She wasn't listening because the baby was crying. So I left for work feeling discouraged and wondering if I should just forget the whole thing.

But on my drive to work, only a few blocks from our apartment, I saw a for sale sign in front of a house. The traffic light was red, so I examined the place for a few seconds and noticed two mailboxes on the front porch and two electric meters on the side of the building. Hmmm . . . I bet that means it's actually a 2-unit/duplex inside. I continued driving to work, with just a glimmer of hope in my mind.

On the way back home that afternoon, I pulled over in front of the house, got out, looked at the listing sign, and typed the listing agent's phone number into my phone. I called as I was pulling into my parking spot at home, wanting to finish the conversation before facing Kelly.

I found out it was indeed a duplex and I scheduled a showing with the listing agent, Dawn Mink.

Perhaps something like this could be what my family needed! I ended up telling Kelly on the day of the showing, and she agreed to come with me. Our excitement quickly dissipated when Dawn unlocked the front door and escorted us in. Although it looked decent from the outside, the inside smelled like cigarettes and cat urine. The layout was funky. And the people living in each unit didn't seem like the type we would want as tenants. In my mind, I tried to figure out how we could "fix it up" enough to be habitable—but I had no context to figure out what to do or how much money it would cost to do it, so the task seemed impossible. It was a no go.

Although it was discouraging, something else important happened that day. Dawn Mink—if you're still out there, thank you. Since Realtors can do this kind of thing, Dawn created an auto-email for me which daily and automatically started sending me every MLS listing categorized as a multi-family home in Bethlehem, PA.

My wife once again demonstrated her persistence (I probably would have forgotten) and checked these auto-emails daily. She breathlessly called me on my lunch break one day in mid-March of 2009.

"You just got sent a listing for a pretty nice-looking duplex," Kelly said. "I already scheduled for us to go see it tomorrow after work." We actually had a friend who was just starting as a Realtor, so we went with her as our representative (Sorry, Dawn! We didn't know any better.)

Immediately upon walking into the building, we noticed a distinct lack of any bad smells. It was a three-story row home, where the first floor had been converted to a one-bedroom apartment and the second and third floors were combined as a two-story, three-bedroom apartment. Both apartments in this duplex had a separate entrance. The seller had bought the building for a very cheap price, and for the last two and a half years, he'd been renovating and living in it. In the three-bedroom unit, where we would potentially live, he had knocked out all of the interior walls so the kitchen, dining room, and living room were open concept. The floors were new tongue-and-groove hardwood. All of the windows were new, double-paned replacement windows. The kitchen cabinets were new. He'd built a second story Trex deck off of the kitchen, with steps down to an off-street parking pad (a huge benefit downtown). He had even exposed an original brick wall in the living room, which gave the place a New York loft sort of vibe. And it was clean and immaculate.

The one-bedroom apartment on the first floor was less ambitious, but it was still decent. Large, clean, with newish cabinets and hardwood floors—it was like a smaller version of our current gem apartment. Best of all, there was already a tenant living in this unit and paying $600 per month in rent. When we finished looking through the place, we could barely contain our excitement.

"We really like it," I said to our Realtor. "We're going to talk it over tonight and I think we want to make an offer."

She told us she would connect us with a mortgage loan officer to get us pre-qualified for a loan.

I spoke with him on the phone the next day, and he asked me all of the standard questions, including how much we had saved that we could use as a down payment.

"About $4,500," I said.

"Oooh, that's not very much," he responded. "I think the only thing that would work for you is a Federal Housing Administration (FHA) loan. It's a 3.5 percent down payment, but the loan is at a fixed rate for thirty years. You'll need to come up with extra money to close, though. Total closing costs would be around $7,800."

The loan officer also helped me figure out what the monthly PITI would be if we could close. He then issued me a conditional pre-approval for a loan. The principal and interest / loan payment total was around $875 (that number is a little high because FHA loans require mortgage insurance), taxes were $225 a month, and homeowner's insurance was $90. That meant we came in at just under $1,200 for our fixed costs. Yes, we would need to pay for utilities—but I figured those would be about the same amount as in our current budget because we were already paying for utilities in the gem apartment. So we would go from paying $825 per month in rent to paying $1,190 in PITI but receiving $600 per month in rent from the first-floor unit.

+	$600	Rent from first-floor apartment
-	$1,190	PITI
	$590	Net personal housing costs

Five hundred and ninety net cost to live in the most gorgeous three-bedroom apartment we'd ever seen. The monthly savings difference would be $335 a month ($825 rent at the gem vs. $590 net cost to own the duplex) at a desperate time in our financial life. The choice was clear, but I still needed a few thousand dollars to pay for all the closing costs.

I took a page out of my old coworker's book and went to my father-in-law. I showed him the numbers I had been crunching. "So, you would save an extra $335 per month by buying this place?" he asked. "I can spot you the extra $3,300 or whatever."

Bingo. I called our Realtor friend, she came over and helped us make all of the necessary decisions on our offer. We told her we wanted to offer the full list price of $175,000.

"I think that's a good idea," she said. "The listing agent told me a few other offers are coming in too."

"Whoa—what?" I began to panic. "You mean we could lose it? I want to offer more."

"Bryce, it's 2009. Nobody is offering over list price," she chided.

"I don't care. I'm not losing this. Please make our offer $177,800." I knew from tinkering around with the online mortgage calculator that this change in price would only add about $100 to our down payment amount and just $10 per month to our P&I. It was probably the single best investing decision of my life.

A day and a half later, our agent called. "They accepted your offer!" she said.

"HOORAY!" Kelly and I danced around in our apartment. I was super excited, but I knew I wouldn't be able to relax until after we actually bought the house. We conducted all of the necessary inspections, got an appraisal, and in late April of 2009, we bought our first duplex. We were ecstatic, and with good reason - it positively changed our monthly finances at the time we needed it most. Here was our new income picture:

+	$2,338	my monthly take-home pay
+	$1,050	Kelly's monthly take-home pay
+	$600	rent from first-floor apartment
-	$305	loss on condo carrying costs
-	1,200	PITI at duplex
	$2,483	monthly budget

This was a big win, but it did not solve all of our problems. The third night we were living there, my pregnant wife and infant daughter were asleep and I was checking my email in the kitchen, standing right under a vent for the shared ductwork in our duplex. I began smelling that pungent, sorta-burned-marshmallow kind of smell that I remembered from the Bob Dylan concerts I had been to. Weed! "Crap. We've got a tenant who is a drug-user . . ."

LESSON 6:
YOU DON'T NEED TO BE A BIG COMPANY TO OWN APARTMENTS

If you were smarter than I was at twenty-three, congratulations! It's not that hard; I was stupid. I'm not sure if I had never really paid attention, or was willfully ignorant—but I seriously did not realize people could make money from something besides their job. I knew people sold stuff on eBay, or started companies, or sold websites. But I kind of thought they went to college to get degrees for that stuff. I knew people made money in the stock market, but I wasn't sure how. I also knew that apartments existed, but I had never lived in one. I grew up in Suburbia. My college had four-year dormitory housing, and I went straight from college back home with my parents. Chandler and Joey from Friends lived in an apartment, and so did Kramer and Jerry on Seinfeld. But the idea of an individual person owning an apartment was as implausible to me as the plotlines of those sitcoms.

The truth is that individual people CAN and do own apartments. At this point, I own thirty-three, plus three offices, and a few parking lots. The key here was what my 23 year old coworker and I both bought, and how we acquired it.

As to the what, most banks will only give the average homebuyer a mortgage loan for residential properties. In the US, residential properties include buildings that have one–four dwelling units. Generally speaking, anything with five units or more is considered a commercial building, and so is any building that includes a commercial space (like a storefront with two apartments above.) So any "normal" person can get the same loan terms for a four-unit quadruplex, three-unit triplex, or a two-unit duplex that they can get for a single-family home, provided they are willing to live in one of the units.

Historically, banks required homebuyers to come up with a 20 percent down payment for the purchase of a home. This means banks also required a 20 percent down payment for duplexes, triplexes, and quads. But the FHA has a loan program which requires borrowers to only pay a 3.5 percent down payment. Banks wouldn't normally accept such a low down payment, but the FHA insures the loan so if the borrower defaults on their loan payments, the bank is not stuck with a bad loan.

This is a terrific loan program for borrowers who don't have a lot of up-front cash, like my wife and me. If we had needed to save up a 20 percent down payment for our first duplex ($175,000 list price), we never, ever, ever could have come up with the necessary $35,000. However while FHA loans can be great, they aren't completely a free ride. The loan is insured—and like all insurance products, there are premium payments. The borrower has to pay a monthly mortgage insurance premium, on top of their principal & interest. For us, this number was around $80 per month. This pushed our payment to $875 (relatively high, given the loan amount). But it was well worth it to acquire an asset that would put us in a better financial position each month.

Most banks, mortgage companies, and credit unions can give you a pre-qualification for an FHA loan amount based on your income, credit score, and outstanding debt. Use this pre-qualification amount to determine what your price point is for purchasing a duplex, triplex, or quad. Call up a Realtor and start looking! Or if that's too scary, get added to an auto-email, the way we did. Most Realtors are glad to sign you up because it requires no additional effort from them after setup and keeps their name in front of you every time a new listing hits the market.

LESSON 7:
LOCATION IS IMPORTANT

In some areas, this housing idea simply will not work—multi-family properties are just too expensive (like San Francisco or Manhattan). In other areas, it won't work because there's not a sufficient demand from a renting population (like most of Montana and Wyoming.) In other areas (American Suburbia), housing stock like this was just never built and often isn't allowed to be built because of zoning restrictions. Both Norristown, PA (where my twenty-three-year-old coworker bought), and Bethlehem, PA (where we live), are fairly densely populated in their own right and are also part of a larger metropolitan area (Greater Philadelphia, Greater NY-NJ-PHL) where millions of people want to live and work. They each have pre-existing stock of properties that are already zoned and approved as multi-family dwellings.

It is important we purchased a home that was already zoned as a duplex.

Today, I rarely look twice at listings for a single-family home located in the downtown area. Even if it could physically be converted into a duplex, I'm fairly certain that I won't be able to get my city to change the zoning to multi-family. And since typically families rent four–five-bedroom homes and they prefer the suburbs (more space and better schools), I can't make a very high-profit margin with downtown single-family homes. On the other hand, there are plenty of young professionals who want to live in downtown Bethlehem, and they don't care at all about the ratings given to the local elementary school. They just want to be able to walk to the restaurants and storefronts.

Many people I have coached and spoken to over the years hear my story and immediately begin thinking about how they could alter their current house by dividing it up into apartments or by buying a large five-bedroom row home downtown and dividing it up, thereby obtaining the same result my wife and I did. In most cases, this won't work. If you own a single-family home, it is probably zoned as a single-family home by your municipality or city. They aren't likely to change the zoning for your home just because you'd like to make some rent money on the side, nor should they. Imagine for a moment if you purchased your dream home in a suburban neighborhood, situated next to similarly built homes. One day, your neighbor decides to convert his home into a four-unit apartment building. A year later, eight cars are parked on the street out front each night, three of them in front of your home. Then the renters are staying up late, playing music, and having parties in the back yard, right next to your kids' swing set. You'd be upset because most of the reason you purchased your home was that it was situated in a neighborhood of single-family zoned properties. So most cities don't just approve a zoning change at the whim of the owner.

If you want to copy this step of our journey, find a growing city where multi-family housing stock exists and is reasonably affordable for an owner-occupant to purchase.

LESSON 8:
DON'T LOSE A GREAT DEAL OVER A COUPLE OF BUCKS

Our agent thought I was crazy when I wanted to offer $2,800 over asking price. I have never offered above asking price since then, and as a general rule, it's probably wise to make low offers.

In 2009, it was considered really dumb to offer above asking price. The entire global economy had been shaken to its core in 2007–2008, and by April of 2009, most people still feared that everything could come crashing down. For investors with cash, it was like a candy store. Everything was priced low, and they could submit ten obnoxiously low offers and expect two acceptances and eight counteroffers. I'm not certain if the competing offers on our duplex were made by investors or by other would-be-owner-occupants, but I stand behind my decision to offer over 100 percent. If I had offered anything less, the seller may have gone with another offer. Buyers who come with an FHA loan pre-qualification, like my wife and I did, aren't the most attractive scenario for sellers unless the offer is high. If two offers are for an equal price, all-cash offers are more attractive for a seller, because there are fewer contingencies and it means inspections, appraisal, and settlement will likely be uneventful. Apparently, the extra $2,800 we offered sweetened the deal enough to make the duplex owner pick our offer. Over the life of a thirty-year mortgage, this $2,800 costs an extra $10 per month. It was well worth it. If we had messed around trying to get the "best deal" possible, we likely would have missed the best deal for us.

Perspective and timing are key too. I had seen and walked through the smokey, cat piss alternative duplex a few weeks prior. My wife and I had also been looking at every multi-family listing that came on the market, so we had a well-developed palate for what constituted a good deal. Timing-wise, this place had three offers within a week of being listed. Even though I was new to the game, I understood that this meant it was probably worth more than its asking price.

When offering on a property that has been listed for forty-five days, you can afford to make a low offer. Chances are, you will be the only offer they are looking at. But don't lowball the deal of a lifetime and risk losing it.

LESSON 9:
ASK FOR A PERSONAL LOAN (THEN PAY IT BACK)

While you're shopping, keep in mind that closing costs will be part of your cost of acquisition. A Realtor, mortgage broker, or loan officer at a bank will be able to help you estimate closing costs well before settlement. In fact, they're legally obliged to do so.

The closing costs on the duplex made it so I couldn't afford it without borrowing from my family. I know, I know—"Good thing you had a father-in-law who was willing to loan you $3,800! Not everyone is so lucky!" We only had around $4,500 to put toward closing, so the rest had to come from family. Closing costs included the 3.5 percent down payment on the FHA loan, an appraisal fee, a payment for a home inspection (a must), title insurance, and various other charges. So, yes, we couldn't have afforded it without the generosity of my in-laws. But I made a great case for it—I showed my father-in-law all of the numbers and even scheduled a second showing for him to walk through the place with us. He could see that we were making a good investment. He also knew how hard we had worked to pay off the car and school loans.

Within seven months of purchasing the duplex, we had paid him back the entire amount by saving our monthly windfall and saving money in other ways while we still had only one kid. We didn't go out to eat, we cut back on travel, and we didn't make any wardrobe purchases. Our quick repayment was important because it wasn't the last time I borrowed money from my in-laws, and it showed I was a responsible person to lend money to.

In retrospect, if my in-laws had been unwilling to loan us the money, it would have been worth it to do almost anything to come up with the extra cash. Selling my car would have been worth it, cashing out the needed $3,800 from a 401k and taking a penalty would have been worth it. Even selling a kidney would have been worth it. At the time, I had no clue what a "hard money loan" was, but it certainly would have been worth it to take hard money in order to close. That duplex changed our lives forever. It was an absolutely indispensable first step.

LESSON 10:
OWNING PROPERTY LOWERS YOUR TAXES

As I shared, this move changed our cash flow by around $325 each month. That doesn't sound like a huge change, even for a sixth-grade teacher. But it was much better than it appears at first glance. For now, I will skip all of the downline benefits that we accrued in future years. But even if we just look at the year in which we bought it, the real benefits are tremendous.

Let's begin with the tax benefits. When you are a tenant, rent is not a tax-deductible expense. A teacher who is making $49,000 per year and renting pays the IRS based on the tax rate for $49,000 of income. But the IRS allows for a mortgage interest deduction from all homeowners' taxable income. So a teacher making $49,000 per year who owns a home has the total interest portion of their mortgage payments deducted from their taxable income. During our first full year of owning the duplex, we paid $8,586 in mortgage interest. With a salary of $49,000 per year, my taxable income was $49,000 minus $8,586 = $40,414. So my taxes were actually lower that year than the previous year when we rented.

Since the principal portion of our monthly mortgage payment went toward paying down our outstanding loan amount, it is a form of saving money, in a way. A thirty-year fixed loan means the entire balance will be paid off in thirty years, and with each passing year, we owe the bank less and less. Although I didn't count it in our $325 per month improved cash flow, this meant we were also "setting money aside" by making principal payments each month.

The other immediate tax benefit comes in the form of additional deductions and assumed depreciation, which I never fully understood until after owning real estate. In short, when the IRS calculates the taxable income for anyone engaged in business, they don't tax the individual based on total revenues; that would be unfair. Instead, they tax them on revenues minus expenses, which is the true measure of how much money a person has made. It's the same when you own real estate that you rent out as a business.

For example, if someone has a lemonade stand and they sell $100 worth of lemonade, but the lemons, sugar, water, cups, and pitchers cost $40, then that individual didn't make $100 selling lemonade. They only made $60. But before being taxed on $60 of profit, a shrewd business person would also argue that they had to pay for the gasoline they burned on their way to the grocery store, $5. Now their taxable profit is only $55. But what about the stand itself? What if that cost $50 to build? Does the individual get to deduct $50 from their remaining $55 in profits, resulting in only a $5 taxable profit for the year?

The answer is no, of course. Chances are, the individual won't need to buy and build a new stand every year. If we assume the lifespan of a lemonade stand is five years, then the lemonade seller will only have to spend $50 every five years to replace it. The IRS looks at this scenario and spreads the $50 cost equally over the five years, resulting in a $10 "cost" for the stand each year. All other things being equal, each tax year the stand owner could deduct $10 in depreciation of equipment from their $55 profits, and their taxable profit becomes $45.

Rental real estate works the same way. Once you own it, you are engaging in business. The IRS does not tax you on your total rental revenues; that would be unfair. Instead, they allow you to deduct costs from your taxable profit in a similar way to the lemonade seller. If you spend money on gasoline to mow your lawn, that cost can be deducted from your taxable profits. The cost of a new furnace (year two at our duplex), the water bill, exterior lighting electric bill, rock salt, hedge trimmers, and washer/dryer repair are also "costs of doing business." This is a HUGE benefit that is not available to the average single-family homeowner because these items are not a cost of doing business when you simply do them around your own home. So as duplex owners, we only got to claim half of these costs as deductions since only one-half of our home (the rental portion) was engaged in business. Still, these purchases were necessary for our living environment, while simultaneously reducing our taxable profits a great deal right away.

On top of that, we got to claim a depreciation loss in the same way that the cost of the lemonade stand is spread over five years. Most houses don't need to be replaced every five years, but there really isn't an exact number of predictable years that houses last. Some last 250 years, some last 35, some last even less. The IRS picked 27.5 years as the assumed lifespan for residential real estate. This means that each year, an owner of rental real estate is allowed to treat 1 / 27.5 of the purchase cost of the asset as a tax deduction each year. For us, this depreciation allowance meant we could claim around a $2,625 deduction in taxable income each year we lived in the duplex.

The real "cheater's edge" in claiming a depreciation loss is that over the course of 27.5 years, most real estate actually gains value. Because of wear and tear, the $50 lemonade stand is probably only worth $40 after one year of use, $30 after two years, etc. But go back and check the prevailing values of homes, duplexes, triplexes, or quads a quarter-century ago—in almost every market in the United States (you'd be hard-pressed to find an exception), values and prices have doubled, tripled, quadrupled or more. Yet during those years of tax-free appreciation, the owners of these assets were allowed to claim that their assets were losing value under the allowable depreciation deduction.

So even though we had more money in our pockets each month after buying the duplex, we actually had a significantly lower taxable income and received a substantial refund as a result.

OBJECTIONS

At this point, you might be thinking that while it sounds great in theory, it won't work for you because [insert objection here]. When I am coaching individuals who are interested in real estate, they often have a number of barriers set up in their mind for why it won't work for them.

1. "What about reserves? Shouldn't I have extra money set aside to handle unforeseen repairs or failures?" If you have that money, terrific. If you don't have that money, it shouldn't stop you from moving ahead with the kind of deal we had lined up. The roof may leak, the furnace may fail, a pipe might burst. These things DO happen. But if you have paid for a professional property inspection prior to closing, you should have a pretty good idea of potential problems. Within our first two years, the furnace failed and our original cast iron waste line cracked in the basement. So we paid for it! We were able to because of the financial difference we obtained by moving into the place. Almost every HVAC contractor and roofer has financing options available, often with 0 percent interest for a year or so. If you end up having an unexpected repair that you can't pay for with cash-on-hand, you can pursue plenty of options. What you CANNOT do is go back in time and acquire a good deal on a duplex that you didn't purchase—it will be gone! And with it, your opportunity to begin making rental income will also be gone.

2. "All of the multi-family properties around me are in a bad area, or smell like cigarettes and cat piss." Keep looking. Knowing what is out there will help you spot a good deal when it surfaces.

3. "The multi-family units around me are too expensive to accomplish what you are describing." Perhaps. Remember, this will not work everywhere. If you are young and single, you may be able to achieve similar profits to my wife and me through buying a single-family home and renting out to roommates. It's a little trickier since you'd be sharing living space with them, but it shouldn't keep you from beginning your investment career.

4. "What if my tenants smoke weed in a duplex that has shared ductwork, and I have an infant daughter and a pregnant wife?" I'm glad you asked. Keep reading.

OPTIMIZING

"**O**ur tenant was definitely smoking weed last night, inside the apartment," I told Kelly the next morning. "I know it's not a huge deal, but..."

"But it's illegal and it reeks and he's doing it inside of the investment on which you've staked a good portion of our financial future!" she reminded me. "He absolutely cannot do that here."

I agreed to talk with him. After an uncomfortable interaction, he texted me later to inform me that he was giving his thirty-day advanced notice for moving out.

"Look at this!" I said to Kelly. "Crap! There goes our $600! How the heck are we going to afford our mortgage and everything else without getting rent?"

Kelly was unfazed. "Heck with him! We didn't want him as a tenant anyway. We'll find someone else; $600 is actually pretty low for a one-bedroom downtown. I know because I looked at so many listings last year. I will take pictures as soon as all of his stuff is out, and we'll create an ad on Craigslist."

That's exactly what we did. The tenant finished moving out ten days before the end of the month. We cleaned, took pictures of the apartment, and created the listing—except we advertised it at $700 instead of $600.

Immediately, I started getting calls from people interested in renting the unit. We scheduled all of the showings for one weeknight and then had people come and tour. Four different people all arrived at once, three took an application, two of them returned the application, and we selected tenants two days later. We used the same boilerplate lease we had used for our condo; I simply changed the relevant details. They signed and began July 1, without us experiencing a single day's vacancy.

In addition to getting rid of a tenant who was a recreational drug-user and replacing him with non-drug–using tenants, we added another $100 of monthly income to our financial picture by increasing the rent. Aside from a thorough cleaning, we hadn't even done anything to improve the unit. In June and July of that summer, I took two courses toward my master's degree in education. This moved my salary higher by about $80 per month starting at the beginning of the school year.

Kelly once again negotiated with her employer so she would be able to continue working even after we had the second baby, so we wouldn't be losing any of her salary.

Now our housing costs looked like this:

+	$700	Rent
-	$1,200	PITI
	$500	Net monthly personal housing costs

And our total financial picture looked like this:

+	$2,418	my monthly take-home pay (+$80 raise)
+	$1,050	Kelly's monthly take-home pay
-	$305	loss on condo carrying costs.
-	$500	Net monthly personal housing costs
	$2,663	monthly budget

This was a happy picture. With respectful tenants in place, a gorgeous apartment with room for two babies, no more master's courses that summer, and a few weeks left before the beginning of school, I should have relaxed. Instead, I decided to get my real estate license! Lucky for me, there was a real estate school located in a shopping center ten minutes from our house. They offered a two-week course. I took it, passed the course, and signed up for the state licensing exam in late September.

The exam date was on a Saturday, and I studied and reviewed my materials for the two weeks leading up to it. Kelly's due date was the week after, and I figured I could have everything finished up before the new baby arrived. I was wrong. My second daughter, Daisy, arrived early, in the late hours of the day before my exam. I slept a total of two hours, made sure Kelly and the baby were OK, and left them in the capable hands of the nurses and my mother-in-law while I drove to the testing site to take my exam. I barely passed, but by the end of October 2009, I was a fully licensed real estate agent in Pennsylvania.

Since I already knew the building well, I started acting as an agent for other landlords in the luxury condominium complex where we still owned our one-bedroom condo. Although Kelly and I had rented our own unit out, it seemed like most other owners wanted to use a Realtor. Every time I found a tenant who ended up signing a lease, my portion of the commission was typically $250. I averaged one transaction per month, which actually brought our monthly lifestyle budget to a level higher than when we had been newly married. These extra earnings allowed us to save a little bit, but were also necessary to cover the added lifestyle costs of two small daughters.

That school year, aside from taking six more credits toward my master's degree in the spring of 2010, we were able to relax a little and just work on being a family for a year. But Kelly's work schedule was not ideal for someone raising two young girls. As our daughters began crawling and walking, I began pondering how to make enough extra money to allow her to fully quit her job. This desire was accelerated in early 2011 when we found out we were pregnant yet again! We decided there was absolutely no way she could continue working because by August of 2011, we would have a three-year-old, a two-year-old, and an infant.

In the spring and summer of 2011, four critical shifts occurred that ultimately allowed Kelly to retire before we had our third child, Lydia, in August:

First, interest rates were lower in 2011 than when we had purchased our duplex. I contacted a local bank and applied for a refinance. The new loan was at a lower rate and was not an FHA loan, which meant we would no longer be paying mortgage insurance each month. The combination of these factors lowered our monthly mortgage payment by over $100, to $750.

The second shift was initially a cause for concern. Our tenants informed us that they would be moving in June of 2011. However, we had sufficient time to advertise the apartment, conduct showings, and sign a lease with a new tenant—for $800 per month, $100 higher than the previous rent. Now our housing costs looked like this:

+	$800	Rent
-	$1,100	Principal & Interest ($750), Taxes ($260), Insurance ($90)
	$300	Net monthly personal housing costs

The third shift pertained to our luxury condominium. It was still rented out, and we had been losing $305 per month for the last two and a half years. But the initial five-year fixed interest rate was expiring, and I worried that our payments would increase. Instead, our rate dropped by 1.75 percent when the five-year term expired. I had never read the fine print in our mortgage docs—which specified that each year after the five-year term, the rate would adjust based on prevailing interest rates. Since these rates were now lower, our payment was lowered by $150 per month!

The fourth shift was that I completed my remaining credits for my master's degree in the summer of 2011, which meant I was due for another $100 per month raise starting in the fall. So our total prospective financial picture looked like this:

+	$2,518	my monthly take-home pay (+$100 master's degree raise)
+	$0	Kelly's monthly take-home pay (No more job)
+	$250	my average monthly commission for rental units
-	$165	loss on condo carrying costs. ($150 lower mtg payment)
-	$300	personal housing costs (+$100 rent increase, $100 lower P&I)
	$2,303	monthly budget

By the time we had our third daughter, Lydia, in August of 2011, we could afford for my wife to cease salaried work completely even though we were below my original functional baseline amount of around $2,700 per month.

Luckily, we had a surprising realization: the costs associated with our monthly lifestyle budget actually decreased after she stopped working.

That year, we relaxed a bit and devoted ourselves to parenting. But I also began to consider two looming issues. First, we wanted our daughters to eventually attend a different elementary school than our duplex location permitted. Second, the neighboring triplex had tenants who were rude, used drugs, and engaged in late-night screaming matches. But what power did I have to control these things?

LESSON 11:
GET RID OF BAD TENANTS

I panicked so much when my tenant said he wasn't going to renew! I had a good reason since our financial survival depended so heavily on that extra $600 per month. Despite those fears, my wife was right to pursue confrontation—and she rightly perceived that we would be able to secure better tenants for a higher rent. In the beginning, this seemed like a huge gamble. However, I have learned that tenants who are willing to break the law (smoking marijuana was and is illegal in Pennsylvania) are probably not going to be good tenants. If our tenant hadn't left on his own, then we would have informed him that the lease was being terminated due to a breach on his part (my leases include a no-smoking clause and an abide-by-laws-of-city-and-state clause.) Now that I've been doing this for eleven years, I've built some reserves and higher profit margins into my overall business—so I'm not at the "mercy" of a $600 loss in rent if that is what it takes to get rid of a problem tenant.

Any landlord who wants to endure should take the same approach. Presumably, investing in real estate should increase the quality of your life, not decrease it. Dealing with drug-using tenants is not my idea of a good time, and the problems they create and attract end up sucking up more and more of a landlord's hours. Since the monthly rent is a fixed amount, tenants who require a lot of time are actually decreasing a landlord's hourly wage, which is not an ideal compensation trend.

LESSON 12:
INCREASE RENT IN BETWEEN TENANTS

To an existing tenant, increasing the rent feels like a punishment. They are likely to be offended by a rental increase or demand an explanation. If you increase the advertised rent between tenants, however, there is no argument—especially when multiple applicants want to rent.

Bethlehem, PA, is a fairly tight rental market. There is a high population density and high demand. People want to live within a walkable distance of the gorgeous and historic downtown, and there are only a finite number of available apartments. So I frequently have multiple applicants for a single apartment even after raising the price. Supply and demand dictate what price the market will tolerate, and there's nothing wrong with trying to find that sweet spot. The best time to try is when seeking a new tenant. Make sure to pick a rental market that supports such gains—once again, this won't likely work in the middle of Montana.

LESSON 13:
REFINANCE OUT OF AN FHA AS SOON AS POSSIBLE

Although an FHA loan is a great tool for acquiring real estate with a low down payment, the loan itself is expensive on a monthly basis because of mortgage insurance. Where possible, it makes sense to refinance out of the FHA loan while still living in the unit, to lower the overall monthly payment to the bank or mortgage company.

In our case, mortgage insurance was $83 per month. This premium is charged every month until the borrower pays down the balance enough to reach a loan-to-value (LTV) ratio of 80 percent—meaning that the outstanding principal balance is 80 percent of the value of the home.

Our 3.5 percent initial down payment had been $6,223, which meant the beginning principal balance for our loan was $171,577. Over the course of twenty monthly payments, that principal balance had been paid down to $169,100—not nearly low enough to equal 80 percent LTV on the original purchase price of $177,800.

But the market had helped us out in a few ways. First, interest rates dropped from 4.75 percent to 3.75 percent over that twenty-month period. Next, home values had also begun to climb in downtown Bethlehem, and we had fixed up our units nicely and were earning decent rent. When we sought a refinance loan, our duplex's appraisal came back at a value of $191,000. Although it's uncommon, the local bank offered a special 90 percent LTV loan with no mortgage insurance. They loaned us $171,000. Of that sum, $169,100 paid off the existing FHA loan, ~$900 paid for closing costs, and $1,000 cash went into our pockets. Not bad, considering it also lowered our monthly payment by around $100.

It's important that I found a local bank to do this. Most bigger national banks do not have a similar 90 percent LTV loan program. If we had tried to refinance through one of them, we would have had to wait until our LTV was 80 percent—and surely would have missed the opportunity to lock in this rate.

LESSON 14:
STEER CLEAR OF AN ADJUSTABLE RATE MORTGAGE

In general, these are a bad idea. An ARM has a fixed interest rate for a short period (our ARM on the luxury condo was a five-year term) and then can go up or down after the initial period expires. Borrowers can get caught with an increasing interest rate which hikes up their monthly payment. If they can't afford this increased payment, their bank can foreclose on the loan. Most banks don't even offer them anymore because ARMs were the source of so much destruction in 2007–2008. Avoid them. We were lucky that when our five-year fixed-term expired, our rate dropped because it was tied to the US Federal Reserve rate, which also dropped and stayed low from years five–ten on our loan.

Conversely, in years eleven–fifteen, the rate has increased along with the rising Federal Reserve rate. I can afford it now, but it would have ruined us financially if this increased had occurred earlier.

LESSON 15:
TAKE PROMOTIONS OR PAY RAISES TO FUND YOUR FREEDOM FASTER

———

While you still need a job in order to meet your monthly budget, take advantage of every raise and benefit available. Although early retirement was the ultimate goal, my job was once again a blessing in this instance. My school district paid up front for my master's degree so I didn't need any money out of pocket. The only "catch" was that I couldn't simply quit my job after obtaining my degree—the tuition obligation was amortized at 25 percent per year. So I needed to continue working an additional four years after completing my degree if I didn't want to owe anything back to my district. This coincided nicely with my eventual retirement

Once I obtained my degree, I was automatically given a raise. In most fields, a master's degree would qualify its owner for a premium salary. In education, it means I went from making $50,000 per year to making $52,900 per year. Not superb, but certainly beneficial for a family closely counting its pennies. So look out for ways you can increase your salary and benefits at your current job.

RINSE, LATHER, REPEAT

The episode that clinched it for me was the "Hammock Bob Marley." One Friday afternoon in the fall of 2011, I came home after a long week of teaching sixth-graders. I walked to my front yard to begin mowing the stretch of grass between the curb and sidewalk. In between my property and the neighboring triplex, a tenant from next door had tied one end of a hammock to a road sign and the other end to a tree. He was swaying, smoking weed, and blasting Bob Marley music. Each of these things violated a city ordinance (Bob Marley is fine; the volume was too loud). I began mowing, and the guy never got out of his hammock! I had to duck under the rope in order to finish the job. Over the previous few months, I had also noticed what I thought was drug-dealing activity on the front porch a number of times. The tenants cussed loudly, did drugs, and threw their cigarette butts all over the front sidewalk.

During the two years from 2009–2011, I'd had a few conversations with the landlord for the triplex. He was in his late seventies or early eighties and owned over twenty units in the downtown area. He did not seem to care who he rented to, as long as the rent was subsidized by the Housing Authority (this government entity sends rent checks directly to landlords, which guarantees they don't need to "chase" tenants to collect rent each month).

The next time I saw the landlord at the property after the hammock episode, I approached him and asked if he'd be willing to sell to me, even though I had no clue how I could ever buy it.

"I'd let it go for $225,000," he responded. To me, that seemed like a pretty high price for a place that needed a lot of repairs and came with troublesome tenants. Two tenants were paying $700 and one $800 in rent each month, for a total of $2,200, which wasn't quite enough to support such a price. I told him I would "be in touch," and then I delayed taking any action for a number of months because I had no clue how I would ever come up with a sufficient down payment to purchase the triplex, let alone renovate it to the level where it would attract higher rents and less troublesome clientele.

While the 3.5 percent down payment on our original duplex FHA loan had worked great for us—it meant we could buy an income-producing asset for a low acquisition cost—this triplex would likely be purchased as an investment property, and most banks require at least a 20 percent down payment for investment properties. In this case, it would be $45,000 plus closing costs for this triplex. Banks also frequently charge a higher interest rate for investment properties and often require a twenty-year loan amortization term instead of the standard thirty-year term. These combined factors meant that even if I were able to come up with a down payment, the monthly P&I for this triplex would be much higher than the payment we had in our duplex and would cut into any cash flow produced by the triplex. It would also take me about ten years to save up $45,000, by which point the landlord would either be dead or the triplex would cost way more.

The more I thought about it, the more I realized that the only way to make the deal possible for us was to live in one of the units and to seek owner-occupant financing again. But I had walked through each unit with the landlord, and they were all kind of "crap hole" apartments. The original superstructure was identical to our duplex, but instead of the second- and third-floor being combined into an open-concept three-bedroom apartment, the first floor was a small two-bedroom apartment and the second and third floors were each one-bedroom apartments. Each one-bedroom apartment was cramped and oddly segmented. The small two-bedroom apartment had one bathroom, accessible only by walking through one of the bedrooms.

In contrast to our nicely renovated, open-concept, New York loft-style three-bedroom apartment, the two-bedroom unit was awful and unworkable as a potential living space for a family of five. But if I could find a way to buy the building, I thought, perhaps we can fix it up enough to live in it.

I asked the loan officer at the bank we had refinanced with if they still offered a 90 percent LTV mortgage to borrowers, even if it's not for their first home.

She said they do, but only if we lived in the home as owner-occupants.

I dug a bit further. "If we move out of our present home, can we keep the existing mortgage in place, even though we wouldn't be living there anymore?"

"Yes, you can do that. There's no obligation to change that mortgage."

Those answers were sufficient for the time being. It meant that I could potentially close with a 10 percent down payment, if everything else fell into place.

I decided to pitch an idea to my father-in-law (who I had promptly repaid our initial $3,900 loan to). I spoke with him and my mother-in-law at their home in Bethlehem. I told them why I wanted to buy the triplex and asked to borrow the down payment and probably some money to renovate.

They asked to see it, and I arranged a walkthrough with the landlord for a few days later. Unfortunately, my in-laws' impression of the triplex was the same as mine, yet they had no vision for a bright future like I did.

"You would live in there?" my mother-in-law said. "Where? The two-bedroom? There is NO WAY you are moving my granddaughters into that hellhole! It's disgusting."

"Well . . . we would fix it up first," I offered sheepishly.

"But even fixed up, there's no way you could FIT comfortably in that apartment," she responded. My father-in-law was doubtful too. It seemed like the deal was dead. I knew my in-laws had a Home Equity Line of Credit (HELOC) that they could easily draw against—my plan was to borrow the down money and the renovation money and simply pay them the interest on their HELOC each month. But they were so opposed to the triplex that it didn't seem like I would ever be able to convince them.

Who knows? I thought. Maybe I AM crazy. Maybe this is a terrible idea for my family. But if I can make these numbers work, it will change our financial picture significantly. I decided to reach out for some help. I recalled that a friend's dad from high school in West Chester was a fairly successful real estate developer. As chance would have it, he was also a friend-of-a-friend to my in-laws. I called him up.

"Hi, Tony," I began. "This is Bryce Stewart. It's been a while—do you remember me?"

"I sure do. What can I do for you?"

"I'm looking at a small real estate deal, and I want to run it by someone who has a more sophisticated perspective than I do. I'm going to be down in West Chester this week and I'd like to know if I can take you out to lunch and show it to you."

"I'm game. I can do Thursday for lunch." I took a personal day from work and drove down to meet him. We went out to lunch, and I told him that I planned on treating him to lunch as "payment" for his advice.

"The BIG question I have is this: how does a guy like me get to be a guy like you?" I asked him. He laughed.

"It takes time . . . and risk. Plus a string of good decisions. Show me the numbers for the deal you're looking at now."

I explained the duplex we had acquired, the neighboring triplex, and the potential opportunity to acquire it.

He leaned back in his chair. "The deals I'm looking at usually have a few more zeros after them. But your ratios are good, and this would cash flow nicely if you lived in it to start with. Your kids are pretty young. I think you could fit for a year or so. Then move on—rinse, lather, repeat."

"Will you say that to my in-laws?" I half-joked.

"Sure. Give me your father-in-law's phone number, and I'll talk to them."

"Really? Ok—I'll tell him that you're going to call tomorrow." I couldn't believe Tony was willing to go to bat for me. Perhaps a professional like him could sway their minds.

Tony ended up talking with both of my in-laws via a speakerphone conversation. They brought up every single objection they had mentioned to me.

"It's a hellhole. This is risky. What if the market drops again? The apartment isn't big enough. Old buildings are dangerous. The schools aren't great in this neighborhood." Tony listened to every objection and countered with solid comebacks:

"They can fix it up in a way that adds value. This is the least risky way to invest in real estate. Prices are lower now than they will ever be and so are interest rates. Bryce and Kelly have already learned how to be landlords, so they know what they're getting into. Since this triplex shares a wall with their duplex, they are actually protecting the investment they've already made by improving the triplex. They won't live there long enough for the schools to matter. Bryce's payback plan means you have a very high chance of gaining back the money you would lend them—and if he is paying the interest on the line of credit in the meantime, it's really no money out of pocket for you."

After the conversation with Tony, my father-in-law reached out to me and said, "We can lend you the necessary money from our HELOC."

Score! Now I just needed to get the place under contract. The landlord and I had discussed his desired price back and forth many times, but he stayed firm at $225,000. I decided that just talking with him was not enough. I needed to put paper in his hands.

In March of 2012, I printed out a blank agreement of sale for Pennsylvania, typed in a price of $195,000, filled out all the other details, and hand-delivered it to the landlord. "I need to get approved for a mortgage on this place," I said. "I don't believe it will appraise for any higher than $195,000, given its condition." He signed!

Ecstatic, I told my father-in-law to arrange for a $23,000 draw (10% of my purchase price plus closing costs) from his HELOC and I called the loan officer at the bank we already had a mortgage with. I sent her a copy of our agreement of sale, informed her that I wanted to pursue the same kind of 90 percent LTV owner-occupant mortgage we had on our duplex, and filled out a mortgage application. I also asked her if we needed to move into the triplex immediately after purchase, or if we could fix up one of the units first.

Luckily, we could, so we didn't have to live in it in its current state.

My plan was to purchase the triplex and then gut and renovate the two-bedroom unit so that we could live in it. Once it was ready, we would move out of our three-bedroom unit in the duplex and find tenants for it. Then, while we lived in the first-floor two-bedroom unit throughout the next year, we would renovate the two one-bedroom units and fill them with tenants.

We scheduled settlement for May of 2012 and closed mid-month. The $23,000 we had borrowed on my in-laws' HELOC was sufficient for the down payment and the closing costs. The monthly interest payments on this $23,000

HELOC at 3 percent interest were $58. Our 90 percent LTV mortgage was $175,500 borrowed at 3.75 percent, for a monthly payment of $813. The taxes were $240 per month, and insurance was $90. As landlord, I would have to pay the water bill and common electric bill, which was around $90 per month. All totaled, the carrying costs for the triplex apartment building looked like this:

$813	Principal &Interest
$58	HELOC
$240	Taxes
$90	Insurance
$90	Water & Electric
$1,291	Total carrying costs for the Triplex

However, for the first month I would also be collecting three rents at $800, $700, and $700. The two-bedroom tenant informed me that they would be moving out in July, which was fortuitous because that was the unit we needed to move into anyway. This meant my total rent was $2,200 during the first month. It gave me a net profit on owning the property:

+	$2,200	total rents
-	$1,291	total carrying costs
	$909	monthly profit

But this profit would only last until the two-bedroom tenant moved out. Then we would need to start renovating her unit to make it suitable for my family to move into. We were going to need to move some walls, change the layout, add a new kitchen, new bathroom, new windows, and a new heating/air conditioning system.

On July 1, the morning after the tenant moved out, I started demolition in the two-bedroom unit. I called a trash hauling contractor, and they dropped off a 15-yard dumpster on our rear parking pad. I began personally ripping out the cabinets, flooring, and bathroom fixtures, and then started knocking the plaster off all of the walls. This was incredibly scary to me because although I knew how to break and demolish an apartment, I had no clue how to put it back together again. I began calling and interviewing contractors who would be able to start renovations in mid-July so we could hopefully move in before school started again.

Meanwhile, my wife was purging all of the unnecessary items from our three-bedroom apartment in the duplex. We began boxing as much as we could and moving it next door, into the basement of the triplex. She also started taking showing pictures of our three-bedroom unit, and she created an ad on Craigslist (in 2012, this was how everyone looked for apartments). It seemed audacious since our fixed costs were only $1,100 per month and we were already collecting $800 per month from the first-floor unit, but we decided to price the three-bedroom at $1,425 per month because that seemed like a decent price for a gorgeous apartment. We immediately started getting requests for showings. Two twenty-three-year-old roommates came to see it and said they really wanted to move forward with renting. The only problem was that they needed to move in by August 8!

I selected a contractor who didn't have anything booked for July (this should have been a clue that he was not in high demand) and he began work on the 15th, promising that he could be done in four weeks. Even if this had been true (it wasn't), it meant that the new two-bedroom apartment in the triplex would not be ready for us to move into by the time our new duplex tenants wanted to occupy in August. We reached out to my in-laws (again!) and asked if we could live with them for two weeks. Thankfully, they agreed—although I'm sure my mother-in-law was tempted to say "I told you this wouldn't work!"

The front bedroom in our new two-bedroom apartment (in the triplex) did not need to be demolished or renovated. It simply needed to be painted. So we painted it, piled as much of our furniture as we could into it, and taped the door jambs and sweep so no renovation dust would get in. Everything else went into boxes and into the basement, and we packed suitcases and moved to my in-laws with three young girls for what we thought would be three weeks.

Our new duplex tenants moved in August 8, but we no longer had a tenant in the demolished apartment unit in the triplex. So our housing scenario looked like this:

DUPLEX

+	$800	1 Bedroom Apartment Rent
+	1,425	2 Bedroom Apartment Rent
-	$1,100	PITI: P&I ($750), Taxes ($260), Ins. ($90)
-	$100	Utilities: Water, Electric, Trash
	$1,025	Net Monthly Profit

TRIPLEX

+	$700	Apartment 2 Rent
+	$700	Apartment 3 Rent
-	$1,201	PITI: Principal & Interest ($861), Taxes ($240), Insurance ($90)
-	$90	Utilities: Water, Electric
	$109	Net monthly profit

Although this increased our budget significantly, we tried to keep our spending around the same. I didn't want to take on unnecessary debt, but I violated my own rule and we purchased a four-year-old minivan and financed it for $300 per month. We simply couldn't afford to buy with cash because every single penny was going toward renovations. Plus, being a landlord, doing demolition all day, and moving meant that I wasn't able to operate as a real estate agent averaging one commission per month. So our financial picture was more like this:

+	$2,518	my monthly take-home pay
+	$0	Kelly's monthly take-home pay
+	$0	my average monthly commission for rental units
+	$1,134	net profits on duplex and triplex
-	$165	loss on condo carrying costs.
-	$300	loss on minivan payment
	$3,187	monthly budget

Once again, we had a monthly budget higher than $2,700. With three young daughters, however, this increase was barely enough for us to get ahead financially. We also needed to finish renovating our apartment in the new triplex, and then eventually the other two apartments.

Our planned move-in date was August 15—leaving enough time to move our stuff in and take a breath before the school year started. But we had picked the wrong contractor. Instead of taking four weeks to complete the renovation, the contractor took twelve weeks.

While we should have hired a new contractor halfway through the job; instead, we limped across the finish line with the original guy. His work was completed by mid-October of 2012, and for two weeks, I watched our girls at night while Kelly drove to our new two-bedroom apartment to paint (she's better at this than I am). I informed the second-floor tenant in early October that we wouldn't renew his lease in November so we could renovate, so he moved out from the second floor around the same time that we moved in to the first floor. We unpacked the sealed-up bedroom that had housed all of our furniture and began emptying the moving boxes in the basement of the triplex. By the time we moved in November, the two-bedroom apartment was very gorgeous, albeit small for a family of five.

It now had an open-concept kitchen and living room, gorgeous hardwood floors, granite countertops, a sparkling bathroom, and more.

After moving in, we bought a bunk bed for the girls' room, put the crib next to it, and squeezed all three girls into one bedroom (ages four, three, and one.) This ushered in the hardest season of my life. I got up at 6:30 a.m. each morning, prepped for school, and left Kelly at home with three very young girls. I coached the cross-country team at the middle school where I worked. When possible, I acted as a rental agent for landlords in our old condo building. When I came home each night after work, I helped Kelly with making dinner and putting the girls to bed around 8:00. Then, from 8:00 until (often) midnight or 1:00 a.m., I went up to the one-bedroom second-floor apartment to do demolition.

Next, I interviewed and hired a different contractor, who completed most of the renovations within three weeks, and left the second-floor unit ready for painting. Once again, the end result was a gorgeous open-concept apartment.

When the walls and cabinets were in place, I spent my late nights painting the entire apartment and installing the final fixtures.

By mid-January, we took pictures and started running a Craigslist ad for $950/month. We quickly found a tenant, at which point I hired the same contractor to begin working on the third-floor unit (I had given the tenant notice of nonrenewal sixty days ahead of time). Once again, he finished quickly and I devoted my late nights to painting and installing fixtures. By April 1, we secured another tenant for the third-floor unit at $950/month in rent. More importantly, all of the renovations on the triplex were completed!

The only downside was the amount of money we ended up borrowing to do the renovations. Because the first contractor had charged so much and taken so much time, we were way over budget. Originally, I had hoped to complete all the renovations for around $40,000. In the end, we spent around $68,000. I was very lucky that my in-laws had access to a sufficient amount of capital to lend us this money; otherwise, we would have been stuck mid-renovation.

At this point, we had spent quite a bit of money on this triplex. With closing costs, it had cost us $198,000 to purchase the building. We had borrowed $23,000 of that from my in-laws, and the other $175,000 had been borrowed from the bank, so we had an outstanding principal balance of around $173,000 after owning it for the past ten months.

In addition, I had borrowed $68,000 more from my in-laws to pay for the renovations. I wanted to get them their money back, so I began pursuing a refinance mortgage to replace the existing triplex mortgage. After all the renovations we had done, I assumed the triplex would be worth more than when we had purchased nearly a year earlier.

I went back to the loan officer from the bank who had originally lent us the purchase loan for the triplex. I told her we were interested in refinancing, and that I thought the property was now worth a lot more than when we had purchased ($300,000 was my guess). She started the paperwork and ordered an appraisal, which thankfully came back at $300,000. Once again, the bank was willing to lend us 90 percent of the value of the house, or $270,000. Interest rates had dropped in the early part of 2013 and were at an astoundingly low 3.25 percent.

We completed the refinance and received a new $270,000 loan. $173,000 of that new loan went toward paying off the year-old triplex mortgage, $23,000 paid back my in-laws for the down payment we had borrowed, $68,000 paid back my in-laws for the renovation funds, $2,500 went toward closing costs, and the remaining $3,500 went into our pockets. The new P&I payment was $1,058 per month. In addition, we increased the rents at the adjacent duplex units to $850 and $1595, respectively.

Now our real estate portfolio looked like this:

DUPLEX

+	$850	1 Bedroom Apartment Rent
+	1,595	2 Bedroom Apartment Rent
-	$1,100	PITI: P&I ($750), Taxes ($260), Insurance ($90)
-	$100	Utilities: Water, Electric, Trash
	$1,245	Net Monthly Profit

TRIPLEX

+	$950	Apartment 2 Rent
+	$950	Apartment 3 Rent
-	$1,388	PITI: P&I ($1,058), Taxes ($240), Insurance ($90)
-	$90	Utilities: Water, Electric
	$422	Net monthly Profit

This finally felt like we were "getting ahead" financially. It changed our overall financial picture to this:

+	$2,518	my monthly take-home pay
+	$1,667	net profits on duplex and triplex
-	$165	loss on condo carrying costs.
-	$300	loss on minivan payment
	$3,720	monthly budget

Now, Kelly could stay at home with the kids and we could afford to live and we could save some money every month. But the small, two-bedroom apartment was truly an unsustainable residence for our family, and I began thinking about what the next move could be. This consideration became more urgent one day in the summer of 2013 when we discovered that we were pregnant again!!

LESSON 16:
KNOW YOUR NEIGHBORS

To be honest, I lucked out in terms of neighbors. I could very easily have purchased a duplex right next to a triplex with a landlord who refused to sell to me. If you are just starting out as an investor, be very careful not only to inspect the property you purchase but the neighboring properties as well. Having bad neighbors, or purchasing in a bad neighborhood, might mean you end up with a rental property where no one decent wants to live. If you already own in a not-so-great area—especially if you are a live-in landlord—it pays to know who your neighbors are. It also pays to call the police if your neighbors are doing something illegal. People stop doing illegal things when the cops show up frequently. My wife called the non-emergency line for the Bethlehem Police Department multiple times. Sooner or later, people who prefer doing illegal things realize that the neighborhood is becoming inhospitable toward such behavior.

If you have an opportunity to buy a neighboring building in a scenario similar to ours, investigate it. I made sure to introduce myself to the landlord and to let him know that when he wanted to "get out of the game," I'd be interested in buying. Both Tony (my real estate developer friend) and I recognized the same reality—if I could control who my neighbors were, I could affect the value of the duplex I had already purchased.

LESSON 17:
MAKE A WRITTEN OFFER

The owner of the triplex verbally negotiated back and forth with me, and he seemed very resolute about a price of $225,000. We even sat at my kitchen table, and he wrote down on a sheet of paper what the net operating income (NOI) of the triplex was, and what the prevailing cap rate percentages were in our area (the ratio of yearly income / purchase price), and why he felt he deserved his asking price.

But when I handed him a signed deposit check for $2,000 and a signed, written agreement of sale, I was showing him that I meant business. I am certain he was getting tired of dealing with the problem tenants in the triplex. He didn't have a mortgage, and this was his opportunity to exit with a big pile of cash. I gave him a good reason to drop his price; I didn't think it would appraise for $225,000. I was right; it appraised at $195,000.

If you are an aspiring investor, don't be afraid to make an aggressively low offer. An agreement of sale / offer is an exit door for a seller. When you hand them an offer with a check, you are giving them a path to their desired destination. Most inexperienced investors never bother making a written offer, and never give a potential seller the chance to act.

If you are attempting to buy an off-market deal, like I did, get your hands on a blank agreement of sale for your state. Read it carefully and include reasonable contingencies for your offer—like the ability to obtain a mortgage, the appraisal of the property, and a property inspection. Then, put down an aggressively low offer. You never know when a seller is going to say to themselves, "Well, a bird in the hand is worth two in the bush . . ."

In this case, I was legally obliged to disclose to the seller that I had my real estate license. I told him, of course, and got his acknowledgment in writing. But both of us represented ourselves in the transaction. There's nothing stopping the average person, or aspiring investor, from doing the same. Approaching him on my own saved him 6 percent in commissions that he would have paid to a listing agent, or around $11,000. So he walked away with the same amount of cash he would have gotten if he had listed it for $206,000 with a Realtor.

LESSON 18:
BUY PROPERTIES THAT YOU WANT

———

This is going to sound stupid: if you see a property that you want to buy, try to buy it. I had a very compelling reason to buy the triplex—not only would it protect the investment we had already made in our neighboring duplex but it would change our financial trajectory for good. I tracked down the owner and put an offer in his hands. Most people don't do this, and I can't figure out why. When you see a property that would help your portfolio, go find out what it will take to acquire it! People tend to build obstacles in their mind or operate based on guesses rather than facts.

"I don't even know if they want to sell!" They do, for the right price. Go find out.

"I'm not ready to buy yet" Who cares? This shouldn't prevent you from seeing what they'd sell for. I wasn't "ready" to buy when I asked the triplex owner—I went and figured out HOW to buy after I knew he was willing to sell.

Look for "For Rent" signs. Call the number and tell the owner you're actually interested in buying. They will NOT say "I'm not interested in selling." I guarantee they will say "how much?" Ask how much they need, and if they give you a crazy high number say, "Thank you, I will see if I can come up with an offer. Where should I deliver it?" Then bring the offer, with the price you want, along with a deposit money check, and hand it to them. They may refuse to sign, or they may counter, or they may accept. Any of those results tell you what it will take to purchase the property, which is the information you were looking for.

Every single piece of real estate is for sale if you make the right offer. That doesn't mean you should just submit offers indiscriminately—it simply means that if you want to buy a triplex because it shares a wall with your duplex, you'd be foolish not to figure out exactly what it will take to purchase the triplex.

LESSON 19:
LEARN TO BORROW INTELLIGENTLY

―――

When we moved out of the duplex and into the triplex, we could have qualified for another 3.5 percent down payment FHA loan. In general, you cannot hold two FHA loans at once. But since we had refinanced out of our first FHA loan (and into a conventional loan) while we still lived in the duplex, we no longer held an FHA mortgage. We could have gotten another FHA loan to acquire the triplex and only needed a 3.5 percent down payment.

However, the 90 percent loan-to-value loan which we did use to acquire the triplex carried no monthly mortgage insurance, which is why we chose it instead of another FHA loan. Often, this kind of 10 percent down, 90 percent loan without mortgage insurance is not available at a large national bank like Bank of America or Wells Fargo. You may need to inquire at a local bank, like we did.

What if you want to begin real estate investing, but you already live in a home that you would prefer to stay in? If you don't want to copy our owner-occupant model, consider opening a HELOC on your primary residence to access the start-up money needed to do what we did.

For instance, if you own a home worth $400,000 and your current mortgage principal balance is $213,000, you have $187,000 of "equity" in your home. When this is the case, you can obtain a second loan on your home. The first loan is your primary mortgage of $213,000. But many banks will give you a second "home equity line of credit" (HELOC) that makes more of your equity available to withdraw as cash. If you used this line of credit to borrow an additional $25,000, your home would have $238K ($213K + $25K) in total loans, and the "equity" remaining would be $162,000.

Most banks will only approve a HELOC that brings the total indebtedness up to 80 percent of the home's value. In the above example, this would mean that the maximum allowable HELOC would be $107,000, because the primary mortgage is $213,000. (Since the home's value is $400k, 80 percent is $320K. You already have a $213K loan, so $107k is the maximum HELOC).

So, using your home's equity to begin investing in real estate is only possible if you have a low enough principal balance on your house to allow you to borrow cash through a HELOC. The benefit is that you wouldn't need to borrow from in-laws and could pay down your HELOC at your own leisure.

For me, the biggest financial concern during this year of insanity was the possibility of not being able to reimburse my in-laws. Because we were willing to pay the interest on their HELOC, it wasn't any extra cost to them. But we took the risk that when we went to refinance after renovations, we might not have gotten an appraisal amount high enough to pay them back.

The triplex appraised for $300,000, and we borrowed $270,000 (90 percent) as the new mortgage. That was enough to pay off the original mortgage, plus the down payment they lent us, plus the substantial renovation costs—with only a few thousand dollars to spare. But what if the appraisal had come back at $275,000? This could easily have happened. The new mortgage would have been the same 90 percent LTV, totaling $247,500. That amount could have paid off the original mortgage ($174,000), the down payment and closing costs we borrowed initially ($23,000), and $50,500 of the $68,000 renovation costs. But this would have left us short by nearly $18,000!

In our case, I'm sure my in-laws would have been comfortable keeping an $18,000 balance on their HELOC and continuing to allow us to cover the interest on it until we saved enough money to pay it off. But not everyone is so lucky. Aspiring investors need to plan for the worst-case scenario and make sure that all parties involved (family, spouse, private lender) can still operate comfortably if it comes to pass.

And even though I couldn't have done it without my in-laws' help, my wife and I had quickly and reliably paid off the previous loan we had taken from them, we had proven that we could be landlords, I backed up my projections with expert testimony (thanks, Tony!), and in the end, we were able to reimburse them fully after the refinance.

"DREAM HOME"

After discovering we were pregnant with our fourth child, we were certain we could not continue living in the cramped, two-bedroom apartment in the triplex. During the summer of 2013, we started looking for a "real" home. At the time, mortgage rates were still around 3.25 percent. According to most banks, we could have "afforded" to purchase a suburban, four-bedroom, two-and-a-half bathroom house for $315,000–$450,000 in our area. Because we had paid back the balance on my in-laws' HELOC, I assumed they would be willing to withdraw a balance again in order to lend us a down payment. But after crunching all the numbers, even a house for $315,000 was going to be too big of a monthly burden:

4 BED, 2.5 BATH SUBURBAN HOME (~$315,000)

$1,234	P&I on a $283,500 mortgage (90% LTV)
$133	$31,500 HELOC payment borrowed from in-laws for down payment
$583	Taxes (monthly cost for $7,000 yearly tax bill)
$100	Homeowner's Insurance
$2,050	Total Monthly Housing Cost

We had just finished the process of optimizing our $3,720 monthly budget, and taking on an additional $2,050 payment seemed like too big of a jump. However, we would be moving out of the two-bedroom apartment in the triplex and renting it out, which would add to our monthly income. We took pictures and posted a rental ad for the apartment, listing it at $1,350.

Immediately, we started getting interested parties, so we knew the price point would likely work.

To keep our monthly budget roughly the same, we would need to pursue a new housing cost as close as possible to the $1,350 we would be making in rent—thereby keeping our monthly budget equivalent. When we discovered that our fourth child would be another girl, we realized we could survive in a three-bedroom house. As long as the house was livable in all other ways, our daughters could easily pair up in two bedrooms for the foreseeable future.

We altered our search and began looking closer to downtown Bethlehem, in 1950s era neighborhoods with lower-priced houses. The winner was a three-bedroom, two full bathroom cape. From the street, it looked like it would be far too small. But the interior revealed a rear addition of a huge, open-concept kitchen, a fully finished 1,000 sq. ft. basement, a side porch that had been converted to an office/study, and an expansive brick patio with an in-ground pool. Another deciding factor was the location: three blocks from the elementary school my wife had attended (and loved) when she was growing up.

We purchased for $252,000 in August of 2013, tapping my in-law's line of credit once again for a 10 percent down payment (our prompt and full repayment of the previous balance proved we were a good bet). Our monthly principal and interest payment was $1,011, property taxes were $370/month, and homeowner's insurance was around $90/month:

"DREAM HOME"—3 BED, 2 BATH ($252,000)

$1,011	P&I on a $226,800 mortgage (90% LTV)
$110	Payment toward $26,000 HELOC through in-laws
$370	Taxes (monthly cost for $4,440 yearly tax bill)
$90	Homeowner's Insurance
$1,581	Total Monthly Housing Cost

DUPLEX

+	$850	1 Bedroom Apartment Rent
+	1,595	2 Bedroom Apartment Rent
-	$1,100	PITI: P&I ($750), Taxes ($260), Insurance ($90)
-	$100	Utilities: Water, Electric, Trash
	$1,245	Net Monthly Profit

TRIPLEX

+	$1,350	Apartment 1 Rent
+	$950	Apartment 2 Rent
+	$950	Apartment 3 Rent
-	$1,388	PITI: P&I ($1058), Taxes ($240), Insurance ($90)
-	$90	Utilities: Water, Electric
	$1,772	Net monthly Profit

When school started again in the fall of 2013, I received another salary increase of $40/month. Our new financial picture—with my growing family finally situated in a stable living scenario and my wife at home full time— looked like this:

+	$2,558	my monthly take-home pay
+	$3,017	net profits on duplex and triplex
-	$1,581	housing costs for our home
-	$165	loss on condo carrying costs.
-	$300	loss on minivan payment
	$3,529	monthly budget

This budget allowed us to meet all of our survival needs, save for things like vacation and Christmas gifts, make extra payments toward our minivan loan, and begin to save for the potential of another investment property. Like my former twenty-three-year-old coworker, we were finally "living for free." The profit from our rentals not only paid for our total housing costs but it also put an additional $1,600 per month into our pockets.

We moved into our new house before the 2013 school year started, and I was able to focus on being a teacher during the day and a landlord in the evenings. But because our rentals had been fully renovated, I didn't have much ongoing maintenance to do. And because the units were so nice, we attracted equally nice and respectful tenants—so there weren't any evictions, police reports, or drug activity to monitor either.

This gave me time to be a husband and a father—which was the reason I had wanted to invest in real estate to begin with. And it was timely because in December of 2013, we welcomed my fourth daughter, Anna, into the world. Once again, it was a premature birth—and we brought her home weighing four pounds, six ounces.

I probably should have been satisfied with our circumstances—not many people are able to arrange their investments and work life in a way that pays for a desirable home in a good neighborhood without both spouses needing to work. But I still didn't like the incentive structure in my job, and I still had my eye on the goal of retiring from my teaching job.

After reading the book Think and Grow Rich, I began doing something which was out of character for me: I started keeping a journal. In this journal, every day, I wrote down my chief financial goal—to retire by age thirty-five with $10,000/month in passive real estate income. At the time, it seemed audacious and insane. But in 2009, when we were renting a two-bedroom apartment and losing $300 per month on our condo, simple financial survival had seemed audacious too. I began to think that the same kind of small, achievable steps which had landed us in our own home, living for free, might also be useful in eventually freeing me from the need to have a day job. I kept my eyes open for another opportunity. It didn't take very long to arrive.

LESSON 20:
OPT FOR THE LEAST EXPENSIVE SUITABLE HOME

Robert Kiyosaki, author of Rich Dad, Poor Dad, is one of many real estate and financial authors who make the controversial claim that "your home is NOT an asset." This claim is controversial because from an accounting perspective, your home IS an asset.

In calculating your net worth (which is often done on a personal financial statement), you are supposed to place your home in the "assets" column, along with everything else you own that has value—like cars, jewelry, art, and other salable items. If the value of your home increases, the total value in your "assets" column also increases. Technically, your net worth increases as a result.

The other column on your personal financial statement is "liabilities"— where you list all outstanding debts. Your mortgage balance is one liability, as well as any loans on cars, college debt, credit card debt, etc. As you make monthly mortgage payments on your home, the principal portion of each payment lowers your outstanding debt. Technically your net worth increases since total net worth is the difference between your assets and liabilities columns.

While it's true that your home is and asset from an accounting perspective, it's false from a financial freedom perspective. Your investing and employment life is lived, for the most part, on a monthly basis. Most people get paid twice per month and set aside spending, saving, and charity allocations with each paycheck. The majority of car payments, mortgage payments, subscriptions, utility bills are paid monthly and grocery budgets are often a monthly consideration.

Because so much of life is lived in monthly chunks, I would argue that an investment asset should be defined as "anything that puts money into your pocket each month." An investment liability should be defined as "anything that takes money out of your pocket each month." By this definition, the house you live in is an investment liability because it takes money out of your pocket each month. The sole exception here is if you live in a multi-family dwelling, like we did in our duplex and triplex. These assets provided a monthly income.

Consider the monthly financial scenario of someone who owns a home that has a PITI payment of $2,000 and lives in an area where home values are rapidly appreciating—to the tune of about $12,000 per year over the last three years. This homeowner has seen their net worth increase by $36,000 during this time as the value of their home increased, plus the accumulated, monthly repayment of around $18,000 of the mortgage debt, for a total increase of $54,000 in their net worth. But it hasn't had any effect on their monthly budget! Unless and until they sell their home for a profit, or refinance into a cheaper loan, any gain in equity doesn't affect their monthly cash flow.

For this reason, when you are shopping for a home and trying to build wealth, I would argue that you should try to find the least expensive home that meets your family's needs. In my case, we could have opted for the four-bedroom, two-and-a-half bathroom suburban home that many of our peers were buying. But this would have been an additional $469 per month in housing costs each month, or $5,628 per year in cash we would have needed to sink into our home with no accompanying budgetary benefit. As you will soon see, this extra $5,628 per year was eventually needed to begin saving toward future real estate investments.

LESSON 21:
RECYCLE YOUR MONEY

To come up with the required down payment, we needed to borrow from my in-laws again. This is where it became important that we had faithfully paid them back before. Once again, because they had access to a HELOC, we were able to borrow through them fairly cheaply.

This instance is an example of how building equity in your home actually can be helpful (although not a full-blown investment asset), since my in-laws used their equity to help us make a down payment, and we were able to move out of our two-bedroom apartment and begin collecting rent from it. When the equity stays frozen in your home, however, it doesn't benefit your monthly financial picture until you sell or pay off the mortgage completely.

We "recycled" money by borrowing out of my in-laws' HELOC in order to renovate our apartments, and then repaying them when obtaining a new, higher mortgage on the apartment buildings. Since the increase in total rents more than covered the increase in monthly mortgage costs, we didn't use any of our own money to do this. And because we repaid my in-laws, the opportunity to borrow the same funds existed for future investments. Once again, if you're thinking of investing, but you do not want to move out of your current home, consider using a HELOC on your own home to "recycle" your money.

LESSON 22:
STAY LOCAL

―――

In addition to being far more affordable for our monthly budget, the house we purchased is about one and a half miles away from our duplex and triplex. This meant that when there were maintenance issues, or when I needed to shovel the sidewalks or mow the lawn, it was easy for me to get to the buildings. And since Lowe's hardware store was only a few miles from the duplex and triplex, I could quickly get what I needed. It would be hard to overstate the benefit of these factors. Living close and being able to quickly deal with issues meant that I didn't need to hire a property manager or spend lots of money on contractors to deal with issues.

Tenants have a habit of locking themselves out of their apartments on occasion. Living close by means that I can easily go and let them in—although I started to charge a "lockout fee" for each episode. Last winter, the electrical wiring controlling one of my furnaces failed, and the tenants stopped getting heat. They called me after getting home late from work, and I couldn't get a contractor to come out that night. Thankfully, I keep a few oil-filled plug-in radiators stored in one of my basements. I was able to drive over and give them three; one for each bedroom and one for the kitchen and living area. It meant that they could at least sleep comfortably until I got a contractor out the next day. Another time, a dishwasher started leaking and I couldn't get a contractor to fix it. Incredibly, I had to make three separate trips to Lowe's before I solved the issue—but I would have given up if the Lowe's wasn't two miles away from the property. Issues like this happen all the time. While I'm no longer in a role where I have to respond to these maintenance calls, it certainly helped to live locally when we first started out and margins were slim.

LESSON 23:
SET BIG GOALS

The book Think and Grow Rich has changed my life. I highly recommend reading this book—but make sure you have a Moleskine journal with you when you begin (they are slim and fold completely flat for easy writing!)

For what seems like my entire life, people in positions of authority have been encouraging me to set goals.

I don't WANT to write goals! I always thought to myself. You're just trying to give me more homework! Or, it felt like I was being nagged by a parent, coach, or teacher. The practice of goal setting never appealed to me until I read this book. When I began to view goal setting as custom designing my ideal life, it became much more attractive. Everyone enjoys custom designing their life: choosing the types of vacations that appeal to them, the kind of house they want, and the kind of car they want to drive.

For me, changing the way I thought about my goals gave me the necessary emotional gasoline to get up early, stay up late, and work my butt off. It helped that I had also experienced a bit of success in real estate investing, which convinced me that attaining my goals was indeed possible—if I could just manage to duplicate what had already worked. It seemed audacious at the time, but the author of the book said I wasn't allowed to pick a non-audacious goal. So I wrote down "I want to make $10,000 a month in real estate income." I didn't just write this once, I started writing it every day in my journal, followed by what I believed to be the next steps.

BECOMING A BUSINESS

After getting settled in our new home and welcoming our new baby, I started casually looking at multi-family listings again. Although I still possessed a real estate license, I had shifted it from "active" status (with the accompanying professional fees and satellite key subscription) to "referral" status (which didn't allow me to function as an agent, but allowed me to be compensated for referring business to active agents).

I got an agent from the brokerage where I held my referral license to keep me on an auto-email for local multi-family listings. In February of 2014, I got an email with three new listings.

The first two seemed promising, but the third seemed like a dud—it was a triplex that was completely unoccupied and the listing showed $0 in monthly rent. However, I scheduled with the agent to go and see all three listings. (I couldn't schedule my own showings because I wasn't an "active" agent anymore.)

It started snowing just as we met at the first property, and by the time we left, it was snowing heavily. When we exited the second property, snow had already begun accumulating on the roads. "Do you even want to go see the third?" my agent asked.

"Umm . . . sure, it's on the way back home for me." We arrived at the third property, which actually looked better from the outside than the showing pictures had made it look online. She opened the front door and we walked into a neat, tidy common hallway. The first-floor unit was a two-bedroom apartment—which was fully furnished and also neat and tidy, but unrented.

"Why is there furniture here if it's unoccupied?"

My agent looked at her clipboard. "The listing agent said it's owned by a small graduate school. They offer three-week intensive courses and allow students to stay here for free while they attend the classes downtown."

"So that's why the listing agent showed the rents as $0?"

"I guess?"

We continued to walk through the second-floor two-bedroom unit and the third-floor one-bedroom unit, which were both fully furnished and in pristine shape. In the back yard, there was a two-story garage building with an automatic, double-bay garage door and an office space on the second floor with a second entrance. Both were full of folding tables, office chairs, chalkboards, and desks.

"It seems like they should be listing for more than $179,000," my agent said. I couldn't have agreed more. This seemed like an absolute steal. But how would I afford it? Kelly and I were settled in to our home and done being live-in landlords, so we couldn't use another owner-occupant mortgage to acquire this property. From what I had heard, banks required at least 20 percent down payment when purchasing investment properties that weren't owner-occupied, and I didn't have that kind of cash lying around. On top of that, I would want to spend a little bit of money after purchasing just to paint and slightly modernize the units.

I called my father-in-law. "You're not going to believe the opportunity I'm standing in right now. I know it's snowing like crazy outside, but I just finished walking through a gorgeous triplex with a detached, two-car, two-story garage that needs very little work—maybe just paint. Can I borrow some money again?"

At this point, my father-in-law had learned that I was a serious investor and that I knew how to recognize good deals. He had witnessed firsthand how Kelly and I had successfully navigated the difficulties and details of our duplex and triplex.

He drove out to meet me at the triplex. He too was shocked by the low price. We both knew that an all-cash offer might be attractive enough for the seller to accept an even lower sales price, which would mean an even better deal for me.

"If you can loan me the cash," I said, "I'd like to offer $165,000 and see if they accept. After I fix it a bit and get tenants in, I will seek a refinance loan and pay you back. But I think I should make that offer today—no one else is likely to come see it in a blizzard, but the next person with half a brain who walks through is going to realize what a steal this is."

He agreed and said he could wire me the money later. I instructed my agent to draw up the offer at $165,000 in cash and send it over to the listing agent as soon as possible. She did so that evening, and a day later, the sellers had accepted my offer!

My wife Kelly was a little bit hesitant about the whole thing, so I asked the agent if we could set up another showing just a few short hours after the sellers accepted. She agreed, and Kelly and I met her there while my mother-in-law watched our kids.

When we arrived at the property, three people were standing on the front porch talking. We walked up and discovered that it was another real estate agent with two investor partners. I knew the agent, and he was a pretty accomplished guy. It made me very nervous. Apparently, his clients had seen the listing online during the blizzard and scheduled the showing. The listing agent had not been able to reach them to cancel or inform them that it was under contract! They had just finished walking through, and they were prepared to make an offer.

"Are you guys here for a showing?" they asked. "You might not want to bother—we're making a full price cash offer," one of the partners said.

Every fiber in me wanted to say, "YOU might not want to bother—we have it under contract!" but I resisted the temptation. Instead, I said, "Oh, that's great! We'll take a look anyway—because you never know!"

My agent unlocked the door and we walked into the common hallway. Both Kelly and I had very worried looks on our faces.

"Can they . . . do we . . . is there any way they can get the property away from us? Or can the sellers change their minds once they get a better offer?" Kelly stammered. "Why were they even here if we already have it under contract?"

"No," said my agent. "We have a signed contract. The ink is barely dry on it, but we have a signed contract. Unless you guys somehow pull out of the contract, they can't do anything. My guess is they had already scheduled the showing before the sellers signed your offer."

We walked through the entire building, and Kelly was just as impressed as her father and I had been. Because she had been through the complete renovation of the previous triplex, she had a context for how little work this place needed.

We began our due diligence on the property, scheduling a professional property inspection and an appraisal. But within a week, my agent's boss (the lead broker at her office) called me with some troubling news.

"Leslie explained to me what you are planning to do with the property—how you are borrowing the acquisition cost from your father-in-law and then plan to get a mortgage later. I just want to let you know that you might not be able to get another mortgage. Fannie Mae and Freddie Mac (quasi-governmental agencies that set guidelines for the mortgage industry) rules only allow a single individual to hold a maximum of four mortgages. After four, you have to buy and finance through a Limited Liability Corporation (LLC)."

Yikes! I hadn't known that detail. In reality, it wasn't completely true—even at the time, there were ways we could have acquired the property in our own names. But I didn't really know enough to question the advice of the broker, so I accepted it as true.

This presented a couple of problems. First, I had NO CLUE how to form an LLC or how much it would cost. Second, the agreement we had signed with the sellers had Kelly and me listed as the buyers. If we attempted to resubmit our offer in the name of our LLC it would invalidate the existing offer, which would give the sellers an opportunity to accept a different (and potentially higher) offer from someone else. I was terrified we would lose the deal.

I deliberated for a bit, but decided to go ahead with the first step: I searched online to figure out how to start an LLC. It turns out that part was pretty easy. The state of Pennsylvania has a database of available LLC names, and I picked a name, filled out the forms, and sent them in along with a $90 check. A week later, a letter arrived at my house from the state capital. The first line of the letter said "Congratulations, and welcome to Pennsylvania's business community." I was a business owner.

In the meantime, we conducted the inspection on this new triplex. After scheduling settlement with the buyer, I had my agent call the listing agent to ask if we could switch the contract from my name into my LLC's name.

The sellers agreed! In my opinion, it's because we were already far along in the process of closing, and they wanted to complete the sale. Phew!!!! In mid-April of 2014, a few days before settlement, my father-in-law wired me the $165,000 needed to purchase. I had been saving up enough money with the profits from the other triplex and duplex to cover the closing costs myself, and I brought the total funds with me to the closing in the form of a certified check.

I can remember shaking when the banker handed me the certified check—it was more money than I had ever had in my life! I headed to the settlement office, signed all the papers, and within a half hour, I was the owner of another investment property.

As I began selling all of the furniture that came with the building on Craigslist, I also sought a tenant for the third-floor, one-bedroom apartment at $825 per month. It was already tidy and cute, and I almost didn't need to change anything about it. It didn't take long before we secured a nice young couple as tenants, happily paying full asking price.

In the first-floor, two-bedroom apartment, I paid a contractor to do some renovations. Once completed, I painted the entire apartment and we advertised it for $1,095—then we quickly got tenants. Lastly, the second-floor, two-bedroom apartment needed a new kitchen and new bathroom. We paid the contractor to do the work and quickly rented the apartment out for $1,095.

After emptying the garage, I listed it for rent as well. Because it was a very new, double-bay garage with an office on top, I was able to get an astounding $495 per month from a contractor who needed somewhere to store vehicles and supplies.

I paid for all of these renovations using the extra cash flow we were receiving from the other duplex and triplex—but I also had to put a balance on my Lowe's credit card to purchase some of the materials. The entire renovation took about five months, and by September of 2014, I had a fully-occupied triplex with a rented garage, which meant I was collecting four rents.

But I had borrowed my father-in-law's $165,000 on a "handshake" and a promise to pay him back. Even with the income this new triplex was generating, it would take decades to pay him back that amount. Technically, there was no mortgage on the property because I had bought it using his cash and without using a bank.

So I approached the same local bank we had used to get mortgage loans on our duplex, triplex, and primary home. I requested what is called a Cash-Out Refinance Loan. The difference between this kind of loan and a normal refinance is that when the average person gets a normal refinance, they are usually replacing their current loan with a new loan from a new bank. People often do this because the new bank is offering a lower interest rate than the old bank, and the new loan will mean lower monthly payments.

But when people get Cash-Out Refinances, they are taking on a new loan for a higher amount than their old loan. The new bank will give them a new loan based on the present value of their home, which may be higher than the value of their home when they borrowed the original loan. If this is true, the borrower can pay off the old loan and have extra money given directly to them as cash.

For instance: Mr. Homeowner saves up a $20,000 down payment and buys a house for $100,000, borrowing $80,000 from the first bank to do so. Six years later, he has paid the mortgage down to $66,000, but his local housing market has surged and his home is now worth $150,000. He approaches the second bank because he sees a billboard advertisement for low-interest rates and because he really wants to buy a $20,000 motorcycle but does not have the cash. Just like when he originally bought the house, the second bank is willing to lend him 80 percent of his home's value. Since it is now worth $150,000, the second bank will loan him $120,000. The second bank calls the first bank to verify that Mr. Borrower owes them $66,000.

So when the second bank gives Mr. Borrower his new $120,000 loan, they deduct $66,000 from the loan proceeds and send it to the first bank so the old loan is satisfied and terminated. But the remaining $56,000 goes directly to Mr. Borrower, who buys his $20,000 motorcycle and still has $36,000 in cash leftover! The $56,000 isn't free, though. Mr. Borrower's new monthly mortgage payment will certainly be higher since he borrowed a larger sum and is now paying down a substantially larger loan than he had at first. But perhaps the motorcycle is worth it?

In my case, the first bank was unofficially my father-in-law. Since his loan to me was based on a handshake, and since I paid at purchase settlement with all (his) cash, my LLC owned the new triplex "free and clear" according to the county records and according to the new bank. This meant that if I received a new cash-out refinance, the sum total of the loan would go directly into my bank account. If I was a scoundrel, I could take all of the loan proceeds and head to Mexico. But my plan was to pay off my father-in-law his $165,000 and keep the rest for future opportunities.

I suspected that the appraised value of the triplex would be higher than what I had bought it for. It seemed to me to be worth more than $165,000 when I bought it, plus we had done substantial renovations and were getting terrific rents.

I told the bank that I thought the property was worth around $300,000, based on the rents. The loan officer told me the appraiser probably wouldn't count the garage rent toward the valuation, and he was right—the appraisal ended up coming in at $270,000. The bank was willing to give me a mortgage with an 80 percent loan-to-value ratio, at 4.5 percent interest rate, on a twenty-year amortization schedule. This meant that the new loan amount would be $216,000 at a cost of $1,367 per month. We conducted the refinance in October of 2014, and after paying closing costs, I walked away from the closing table with a $213,000 check and hands that were even shakier than during the purchase!

I deposited the money into my bank and then wired my father-in-law back his $165,000 plus accumulated interest. I paid off the balance on my Lowe's card, paid myself back for some of the closing costs, and finished paying for new gas boilers that provided each apartment with separately metered heat. The remaining sum was $35,000—seed capital for my next investment! In the meantime, I had a new, cash flowing triplex with numbers that looked like this:

NEW TRIPLEX

+	$825	Apartment 3 Rent
+	$1,095	Apartment 2 Rent
+	$1,095	Apartment 1 Rent
+	$495	Garage Rent
-	$1,777	PITI
-	$110	Utilities: Water, Electric
	$1,623	Net monthly Profit

My other housing costs still looked the same:

"DREAM HOME"—3 BED, 2 BATH ($252,000)

$1,011	Principal & Interest on a $226,800 mortgage (90% LTV)
$110	Loan payment toward $26,000 HELOC through in-laws
$370	Taxes (monthly cost for $4,440 yearly tax bill)
$90	Homeowner's Insurance
$1,581	Total Monthly Housing Cost

DUPLEX

+	$850	1 Bedroom Apartment Rent
+	1,595	2 Bedroom Apartment Rent
-	$1,100	PITI
-	$100	Utilities: Water, Electric, Trash
	$1,245	Net Monthly Profit

TRIPLEX

+	$1,350	Apartment 1 Rent
+	$950	Apartment 2 Rent
+	$950	Apartment 3 Rent
-	$1,388	PITI
-	$90	Utilities: Water, Electric
	$1,772	Net monthly Profit

At this point, my family's monthly budget was also altered dramatically:

+	$2,558	my monthly take-home pay
+	$4,640	net profits on duplex and triplex AND new triplex
-	$1,581	housing costs for our home
-	$165	loss on condo carrying costs.
-	$300	loss on minivan payment
	$5,152	monthly budget

This new acquisition had forced me to learn a number of great lessons: how to start an LLC and how to negotiate commercial financing with banks. But most importantly, it taught me that I could create value and even cash "out of thin air" by recognizing an underpriced property, acquiring it, and completing a cash-out refinance. I was walking away with $35,000 in cash and ready for my next acquisition.

I made one mistake, though. Since I was personally removing a lot of the furniture from this new triplex and since I was doing a lot of the landscaping and even purchasing some of the materials our contractor used to renovate the building, I bought a truck. I told myself that I needed it in order to renovate the property and operate efficiently as a landlord. But I saddled myself with a $15,000 loan that had a $300 a month payment. I'm glad that I didn't use any of the $35,000 seed capital to buy the truck, but in retrospect, I should have just rented a Uhaul on the days I really needed to carry heavy stuff and continued to drive the little hatchback I already owned.

LESSON 24:
LOOK UNDER LOTS OF "ROCKS"
(GO SEE PROPERTIES, EVEN IF THEY DON'T SEEM GOOD AT FIRST)

I almost didn't do the showing at the triplex. After all, it was snowing pretty hard that day and the online listing on the MLS showed that the building wasn't generating any income. There were only a few pictures of the triplex online, and they weren't very good. Going to see it could have been a big waste of time. Instead, it was the deal of a lifetime! I bought it for $165,000 and with about $20,000 of renovating, it appraised for $270,000!

Hungry, foraging bears are willing to look under a lot of rocks in order to find food. Any aspiring real estate investor should internalize this lesson—you are usually not risking anything by going to check a property out. It may be a waste of time, and it may be inconvenient. But the more inconvenient the deal is (like during a blizzard), the higher the chances are that other investors will have given up or turned back.

In this case, it was very foolish for the seller's listing agent to create an ad showing the rents as $0 for each unit. She should have put an estimated rental amount in the MLS listing. Her mistake nearly kept me from going to see the unit, because I assumed it was in disrepair or gutted or had some other serious problem that would have prevented someone in my position from intelligently purchasing. The pictures and description in the listing were equally foolish because they didn't highlight the best features of the property. I can only assume that other investors were turned off or at least delayed in arranging a showing—an assumption confirmed by the presence of competing agents and investors on the front porch when we returned for a showing.

It definitely paid to look under that rock!

LESSON 25:
ACT FAST ON GOOD DEALS

———

If I had hesitated for even a day, I probably wouldn't have gotten the deal. I knew it was undervalued at $179,000 and figured I would be getting an incredible deal if the sellers accepted my offer of $165,000. You could argue that I was very lucky to have a father-in-law willing and capable to loan me $165,000—and you would be right. But my request didn't come out of a vacuum—I had already proven myself to be wise, persistent, and able to take projects past the finish line. He had watched me analyze deals and then create value and establish an income stream on our other two properties, and I was no longer inexperienced nor idealistic.

I had also shared numbers with him in the past—he came to understand a lot about our local market through my experiences. So he also had a pretty good idea that the property was underpriced. He rightly assumed that his money would be safe.

However, neither his money, nor my experience, nor the incredibly low list price would have mattered if I had not gotten the property under contract first. You can always find a way to get out of a contract. But what you cannot do is find a way to buy a property that someone else already has under contract. Putting a property under contract actually has very few risks, as long as the agreement has certain contingencies. I included normal and reasonable "outs" in my offer—an inspection contingency, a radon contingency, and an insurability contingency. If I had discovered something in the due diligence phase that was a red flag, I could easily have exercised one of these clauses and walked away from the deal without even sacrificing my earnest money deposit.

But if I had delayed in making the offer by even one day, the competing investors on the porch surely would have gotten their full-priced, cash offer accepted ahead of mine. And then what would my options have been?

LESSON 26:
START AN LLC ONCE YOU AREN'T A LIVE-IN LANDLORD

I already had four mortgages (condo, duplex, triplex, single-family residence) and my agent's broker convinced me that I wouldn't be able to get a fifth mortgage. Yet even in 2014, this wasn't entirely true. Yes, Fannie Mae and Freddie Mac's guidelines had limitations, but many banks could use their own guidelines. Furthermore, Fannie and Freddie have since increased their limit to ten mortgages.

Because I didn't know any better, I simply plowed ahead with starting my own LLC. I knew that plenty of investors started LLCs, but I thought of it as something beyond my own level of sophistication—it scared me greatly and I almost let it intimidate me into backing out of the deal. In reality, starting an LLC in Pennsylvania really wasn't very hard. In most states, it is relatively easy and inexpensive.

Since this experience, I have encouraged many investors to start their own LLC even before they identify the property they would like to purchase. There is no requirement to immediately purchase a property with the LLC. You could wait years if you wanted. But needing to form an LLC in the middle of a deal (like I was forced to do) could waste valuable time and even lose you the deal (my sellers could technically have canceled the contract when I asked to change the entity name, and then gone and found the other buyers who were willing to pay full price). Serious investors put themselves in a position to act quickly so when a deal emerges, they are able to move forward. Start your LLC yesterday.

LESSON 27:
USE THE "BRRRR" METHOD OF INVESTING

I didn't know it at the time, but throughout this transaction, I was instinctively doing what many investors now call the BRRRR method of real estate investing: Buy, Renovate, Rent, Refinance, Repeat. It is a strategy that has led lots of investors to incredible fortunes. For many, it began when they somehow received a large lump sum of money. Perhaps they sold their primary residence and walked away with a non-taxable, six-figure gain. Or they inherited money. Or maybe they liquidated their 401K after working a high salary job for a decade.

The important thing to observe, though, is how astoundingly high the ROI (return on investment) percentage is for this strategy, and then you will understand how it has created so many millionaires. My ROI on this deal was somewhere in the neighborhood of infinity, which I view to be a pretty good investment!

A common way to evaluate most investments is to calculate the annual return delivered by the investment as a percentage of the acquisition cost.

Stocks, as a group, have historically yielded around 8 percent average annual returns on the New York Stock Exchange. This means that $165,000 invested broadly in stocks would pay you around $13,200 per year, leaving you with $178,200 after the first year.

Real estate, as an asset class, has historically appreciated around 3 percent annually. If you were to purchase a piece of real estate at a cost of $165,000, and a year later it was worth around $169,950—you could claim to have gotten your 3 percent ROI (which would be inferior to stocks).

Bonds can often return well below 2 percent, which would give you $3,300 in interest dividends after one year and leave you with $168,300. The interest derived from savings accounts or CDs is usually even lower.

At these rates of return, how long would it take $165,000 to become $1,000,000? Stocks would take around twenty-four years at 8 percent ROI. Normal real estate would take sixty-two years at 3 percent ROI. If you invested that $165,00 in bonds at 2 percent ROI, it would take ninety-one years to become $1 million.

But someone who used the BRRRR method of acquiring rental real estate could become a millionaire much faster because they can continually recycle the same lump of money. In my case, the $165,000 acquisition cost of the triplex was refinanced back out of the deal within six months, so the total "cost" of the acquisition was $0. When I refinanced, I gave my father-in-law his $165,000 back. I got my $8,000 in closing costs back, plus enough to pay off my Lowe's bill, plus around $35,000 in extra money. I also owned an asset that was producing $1,623 in monthly cash flow and around $300/month in monthly principal down payment, or $23,076 per year. On top of that, I now owned around $54,000 of equity in the property, since it was appraised at $270,000 and my beginning loan principal was $216,000. So in total, my first year's "return" from this acquisition was $35,000 cash + $23,076 rents/loan down payment + $54,000 equity = $112,076. In the following years, the two recurring returns were the rental cash flow from my tenants of $19,476, the annual principal down payment of around $3,600 of the loan, and the continued 3 percent annual appreciation of the property ($8,100) for a total of about $31,000 in subsequent yearly gains. For an investment of $0 of my own money, this is an infinite ROI.

It is also a strategy which freed up the initial $165,000 to be used again if my father-in-law was willing and if another wonderful deal showed up (eventually, it did). This triplex with a garage was really good, and I'm not suggesting every deal will occur like this for aspiring investors, but a smarter investor could repeat it three times in a year with similar results (I know investors who have done this). Their $165,000 could conceivably create $122,076 x 3 = $366,228 in added yearly net worth. At such a pace, it would take two years and four months (seven deals) for $165,000 to become $1 million in total net worth, and if the investor stopped buying after this threshold, the portfolio would generate above $200,000 in yearly income thereafter.

Someone who repeatedly borrows the $165,000 (like me) and only does two deals per year could turn $0 into a $1 million net worth in about four years (eight deals), with a yearly income of well over $200,000 if they stopped at eight. There are very few avenues to great wealth which are better and quicker than this method of real estate investing, when done wisely.

LESSON 28:
DIVIDE HEATING COSTS IF POSSIBLE

When possible, it's often wise to divide up the heating systems for an apartment building so the tenants' electric meter or gas meter carries the cost of their heat. This way, the landlord isn't responsible for tenants' heating choices. When people don't pay for their own heat, they have no incentive to conserve or to curb their usage. I have seen (and owned) apartment buildings with a single heating system where the landlord paid for the heat, and the tenants had the windows wide open in the middle of winter! So I divided the heat in this building in order to make sure I wasn't paying for my tenants' heating choices.

When showing potential tenants such apartments, I simply tell them "everyone uses what makes them comfortable, and pays for what they use—that's fair." I've never gotten one complaint about tenants needing to pay for their own heat.

Sure, there are some drawbacks. First, you have to pay the initial cost of installing separate heating systems. It's not cheap. Next, it means you'll have to maintain and possibly repair multiple systems over the years—they will need servicing and may eventually fail. Plenty of landlords skip the initial cost, leave the existing system in place, and just factor the heating costs into their asking price for rent. But this still leaves them vulnerable to cost fluctuation based on tenants' usage. And if a tenant searching on Zillow screens for one-bedroom apartments below $1,000 a month in rent and you've factored heat into your asking price of $1,050, your apartment won't show up on their search.

The other factor to consider is the effect separated heat has on the overall value of the property. Most sophisticated investors will value a property based on its NOI. This number is the yearly profit a property generates, excluding the cost of financing. Investors then assign a value to the property based on the profit it generates. Although this can vary significantly, it is helpful to think of the potential value of the property as being a certain multiple of the NOI (12 x NOI would be a decent multiple). Investors are often willing to buy a property for twelve times the annual NOI.

Consider this overly simplified fictional example. If a triplex property generates $30,000 per year in rental income and has $7,000 in various operating costs and a $3,000 annual heating bill, its net operating income would look like this:

$30,000	Annual Rents
- $7,000	Taxes, Insurance, Trash, Water, Repairs, etc.
- $3,000	Heating costs
$20,000	Net Operating Income

An investor looking to purchase at a multiple of twelve would be willing to purchase the triplex for $240,000.

$20,000	NOI
x 12	Value Multiple
$240,000	Potential Sales Price

If investors in a certain market are generally willing to purchase investment properties at 12 x NOI, the owner of the triplex could reasonably estimate the value of his building to be $240,000.

But if the owner spent $15,000 to remove the existing shared heating system and install three dedicated systems (one for each unit) billed directly to the tenants, they would be eliminating $3,000 of their annual costs because they would no longer be carrying an annual heating bill. Now the NOI changes and so does the value/potential sales price:

$30,000	Annual Rents	
- $7,000	Taxes, Insurance, Trash, Water,	
- $0	Heating costs	
$23,000	Net Operating Income	
$23,000	NOI	
x 12	Value Multiple	
$276,000	Potential Sales Price	

In such a scenario, by making a $15,000 investment, an owner could increase the value of their property by $36,000. Or, while still owning the property, their $15,000 would have decreased their annual costs by $3,000—which is a 20 percent annual ROI. While this calculus only applies to valuations based solely on NOI (and not on comparable sales or "comps"), it is still a significant consideration for investors.

SEED CAPITAL

——

After paying my father-in-law back his $165,000, paying myself back for the closing costs, and paying off the balances on my credit cards for the renovations costs, I had $35,000 left from the proceeds of the refinance. The bank that gave me the mortgage was willing to lend 80% percent toward the purchase of future apartment buildings, meaning I would need to fund the other 20% of any new purchase. The $35,000 would act as a 20% down payment of any purchase up to around $175,000. This gave me a good idea of the price range to beginning shopping, if I was so inclined.

In the meantime, I was beginning to dedicate more time to working on my budding real estate business. Each property had at least a small amount of grass that needed to be mowed each week. Each one also had a common hallway that needed to be vacuumed, and with ten different tenants now (one at the condo, two at the duplex, three at the first triplex, four at the new triplex + garage), around 4–5 move-outs were occurring each year, which meant I needed to advertise, conduct showings, and monitor move-ins and outs to make sure everything got cleaned and nothing was damaged. I didn't necessarily mind the work—but I wondered if I had the capacity to self-manage enough properties to reach my financial goals. I also worried about the risks of continued expansion—it would mean more loans, more tenants, more potential vacancies. But one incident at my school prompted me to continue my path toward financial freedom with great haste.

During this school year, I had a particularly difficult student who was highly disruptive in class. Although certainly capable, the child refused to ever stop talking while other students were attempting to work and refused to remain in their seat. My fellow teachers and I tried every strategy in the book to engage and correct the student, but nothing worked. We finally called the parent and scheduled a conference. When we explained the student's behaviors, the parent responded that this was "just [the student]'s personality."

I was incredulous! This parent had an opportunity to address some serious behavior problems with their child, not to mention make life much easier for other students in the classroom and for the teachers. But the parent refused to correct or discipline their child.

So we began recording all of the disruptive behaviors and referring the student to the guidance counselor's office or to the principal's office. However, the student never did anything quite serious enough to justify suspension or expulsion. This child knew where "the line" was and danced up to the line daily. When I would firmly direct the child to be seated and to stop talking, the student would comply for a few minutes. Then they'd wait just long enough before laughing, yelling, telling a joke, or getting out of their seat so it wouldn't strictly count as defiant behavior because they weren't disobeying a direct instruction. When I would firmly remind them again, they'd respond "What? What did I do? I'm just sharpening my pencil!" (for the fourth time).

In ten years of teaching, I only really lost my temper once, and it was with this student. One day while I was trying to lead an activity on the overhead screen, the student got up to sharpen their pencil (again!) and on the way back to be seated, pretended to fall (I know what a fake fall looks like) and shoved another student's notebook off his desk in the process. Everyone laughed of course, and I told the student to please go wait for me in the hallway. The response I got was "What? What did I do? Now I'm going to get in trouble for FALLING?"

"Get out in the hallway, right now, please!" I said.

I escorted the student out the door, and once in the hallway, they turned around and shouted (so that everyone inside could hear) "ONLY A MORON WOULD SEND SOMEBODY TO THE HALLWAY FOR FALLING DOWN!"

Now, I shouted back, "JUST . . . SHUT . . . YOUR . . . MOUTH!!!!" and I slammed the door closed so hard that all of the safety glass in the door window shattered! When I told my principal about the incident after the period was over, she told me that I would be paying for the replacement of the safety glass pane.

At the end of that school day, I wrote in my planner, "I will not endure this for the next thirty-five years. I must, must, must work myself out of this job."

Thankfully, I had $35,000 in the bank and I was still on my real estate agent's auto-email list for multi-family listings in Bethlehem, PA. In November of 2014, I received a listing for a decent-looking duplex in downtown Bethlehem, priced at $160,000. It had a detached, two-car garage—which I now had experience in renting out since the triplex had a garage as well.

We went to go see the duplex, and it was in pretty decent shape. The owner lived in the first-floor apartment. He was an airline pilot, and he was moving because he had been hired by a bigger and better-paying airline in Texas. While living in the duplex, he had installed motion lights for the entire exterior of the building, he took decent care of the lawn in the back, and he had been fairly conscientious in the general upkeep of the place.

I instructed my agent to draw up an offer (in my LLC's name) for $150,000. The seller made a counteroffer of $154,000 and I accepted. I knew that I would be able to use my $35,000 as a down payment, with enough extra money to cover all of the closing costs and about $1,000 to spare. We conducted all of the due diligence (inspections and appraisal) and nothing was out of the ordinary. To meet the contract deadlines, we had to schedule settlement for January 2, 2015. I recall driving home from a family reunion late on the night of New Year's Day so I could make it to settlement early on the morning of the second. But it was worth it, and I closed on another terrific property. When it was fully rented, the numbers looked like this:

NEW DUPLEX

+	$850	Apartment 1 Rent
+	$950	Apartment 2 Rent
+	$290	Garage Rent
-	$1,087	PITI: Principal & Interest ($747), Taxes ($250), Insurance ($90)
-	$100	Utilities: Water, Electric, Trash
	$1,003	Net monthly Profit

In addition to this acquisition, a few months later I paid off the remaining balance on our minivan. I also raised the rent by $50/month when turning three of our other apartments around. These items changed my family's monthly budget as follows:

+	$2,558	my monthly take-home pay
+	$4,640	net profits on duplex and triplex and new triplex with garage
+	$150	increased rent in first duplex and first triplex
+	$1,003	net profits on new duplex
-	$1,581	housing costs for our home
-	$165	loss on condo carrying costs
-	$300	loss on truck payment
-	$0	loss on minivan payment
	$6,305	monthly budget

Given that this amount was much higher than what we were accustomed to living on, I was really able to begin stashing money away. My total real estate income was $5,658 per month—which was much more than I was making at my job—it also convinced me that achieving my completely audacious goal of early retirement and eventually "$10,000 a month in passive income" was possible, and I was over halfway there.

LESSON 29:
USE CURRENT DISSATISFACTION AS FUEL FOR MOTIVATION

I know that the initial scene where my principal squandered my hundred hours of time seemed like it was the "watershed moment" for me. In truth, I had a couple of watershed moments. My experience with this student was certainly one of them. But these things drove me to make concrete plans and begin to take concrete actions. Perhaps you are in a similar situation.

My encouragement is to use the indignities, frustrations, and perhaps a dead-end job as fuel for your quest toward financial freedom. Write down what you want and what you're willing to work toward, and begin taking the steps you are able to right now. When you are tempted to neglect writing lists down, or making a phone call, or sending an email, or filling out paperwork—remember your frustrations and temporarily channel your anger toward the constructive completion of a task that forwards your goal. This habit adds up over time and becomes the very vehicle that carries you to freedom.

LESSON 30:
BUY A "TURNKEY" PROPERTY

The duplex I bought in this chapter was in better shape than the other units at the time I had purchased them. However, since I renovated the other units, this one wasn't as updated. The paint colors were drab and the kitchens and bathrooms were a bit dated, but it didn't smell like cigarettes or cats, and it was clean and reasonably landscaped. It also came with paying tenants on the second floor and a one-bedroom apartment on the first floor that was immediately ready to be advertised and rented. The garage also rented quickly.

I have certainly benefited by adding value to my properties through intelligent renovations. But in finding a place that was undervalued to start with, I saved myself a lot of work and a lot of renovation costs. When possible, push forward with these deals. It eliminates the risk and effort of renovations.

9

THE FINISH LINE?

—

Kelly and I began saving our extra income while continuing to live on around $2,700 per month. In the summer of 2015, I had officially worked four full years since finishing my last credits toward my master's degree. Since my district amortized this "tuition loan" over a four-year term, it meant that I could quit my job without owing them any money back for my master's degree. But I didn't have to quit.

Two unfortunate announcements came to me via email that summer. First, for budgetary reasons, the school district was freezing my salary, as well as every other district teacher in the eight–ten year salary step. Second, our district employee health insurance plan was being restructured, and we would be paying a higher amount of our paychecks toward the plan. This meant that if I returned to work in the fall, I would officially be taking home a smaller paycheck each month. I didn't like that prospect.

Although I wasn't completely certain that I wanted to retire, I called PSERS (Pennsylvania State Educators Retirement System) and asked what the process looked like for retiring early. I had been paying into the pension fund for ten years, and I was vested—which meant I was entitled to a small monthly pension income as well as the ability to withdraw the cumulative total of my contributions over the years. Neither number was impressive, but it was better than nothing. I filled out all of the necessary paperwork, but I didn't send it in. I knew I would need one more rental property in order to meet our family's budget and still have enough cushion left over to pay for our own healthcare and to buffer against unforeseen costs.

It was in the midst of these processes that I received an auto-email from my Realtor with a decent-looking listing for a triplex in Bethlehem.

We went to go see the building, and I was not initially very impressed. One of the units was a one-bedroom and smelled heavily of smoke. A two-bedroom unit on the first floor was decently sized and had exclusive access to the basement. However, the entire unit was full of the tenant's belongings, almost from floor to ceiling. The third unit was a smaller, walk-up, one-bedroom apartment—barely big enough for one person but inhabited by a couple.

The heating system was a shared system—cast iron radiators all tied into an oil boiler. This was undesirable for a few reasons. First, I didn't want to be paying for my tenants' heating choices, just like in the other buildings. Second, oil has to be delivered to a tank in the basement, which fuels the boiler. Aside from visually checking the tank, I wouldn't know how much oil was left at any given time, meaning the oil could run out without my knowledge, so I would need to regularly check the tank's gauge during the wintertime.

It also looked to me like parts of the roof needed to be repaired. There was a large shed attached to the back of the building, which would normally be an asset. But it was full of obsolete supplies and tools from decades of landlording—most of it predated the current owner. Overall, though, it would generate a tidy profit for me each month if I were to purchase. I could always begin fixing the aspects I didn't like in subsequent years.

List price was $205,000—but I knew I would need to price a number of repairs and remedies into my offer. The rents weren't stellar ($925, $850, $500), but I believed they were under market and could be raised. Once again, I called up my father-in-law.

"I'm wondering if I can utilize your line of credit again," I said to him. "I found what I believe to be a decent triplex, and I'd like to offer them $195,000 cash."

He said he could do it, so I requested another showing through my agent. My father-in-law walked through with me, and when we finished, he was even more optimistic than I had been.

"This place is bigger than your other triplexes," he said. "If done right, it could bring in even more money than the others. Hopefully, they'll accept your offer!"

Later that day, I instructed my agent to prepare an offer for $195,000 in cash (once again, I was purchasing through my LLC). I signed it and she sent it to the seller's agent. I waited overnight before getting a response. The next morning, my agent called me.

"They accepted your offer!" she informed me. "Let's schedule your inspections." I didn't bother to schedule an appraisal because I knew I would be bringing my father-in-law's cash and because I knew what my other triplex (a few blocks away) was worth, which was a good comparable property.

A week later, the inspection revealed what I had surmised—a significant portion of the roof needed to be repaired. I called a local roofing contractor and got them to come out and give me an estimate while I still had time within my contingency window—and he gave a price of $6,000.

With all these repairs, I knew I needed to modify my offer. I requested a $7,000 reduction in price for the roof and for anticipated clear out costs for some of the shed garbage, and I gave my agent a copy of the roofing estimate to forward to the sellers. After thinking it over, they grudgingly agreed to the reduction. Our new sales price was $188,000, and we scheduled settlement for August 14, 2015.

I began doing the rough math for this acquisition, and what it would mean for our income picture:

$850	1 bedroom apartment
$925	2 bedroom apartment
$500	1 bedroom apartment
$2,275	Total Rents

The monthly costs looked like this:

$1,150	Projected Mortgage, after refinancing and paying my father-in-law his $188,000
$375	Taxes
$100	Insurance
$70	Water
$20	Trash
$200	Heating Oil Averaged Over 12 Months
$1,915	Total monthly costs

This meant I'd have around $360/month in net profits, which really wasn't very high. But I knew that I could separate the heat and that the rents were below market. Given the profitability I had achieved in my previous triplexes, I was confident I could get the same profits at this property, eventually.

In mid-August, we closed on the triplex—my sixth rental property! I spent a few thousand dollars right away to fix the roof and to separate the heat by removing all of the radiators and hiring an electrician to install baseboard electric heaters, controlled individually by each tenant and billed to their electric meters. The $500 lease expired, and I increased the lease amount to $550 and rented to a new tenant. This increased my monthly profits to $610 and brought my overall financial picture to this:

"DREAM HOME"—3 BED, 2 BATH ($252,000)

$1,011	Principal & Interest on a $226,800 mortgage (90% LTV)
$110	Loan payment toward $26,000 HELOC through in-laws
$370	Taxes (monthly cost for $4,440 yearly tax bill)
$90	Homeowner's Insurance
$1,581	Total Monthly Housing Cost

CONDO

+	$1,095	Rent
-	$242	Home Owner's Association Dues
-	$300	Taxes
-	$718	Principal & Interest
	$165	Net Monthly Loss

FIRST DUPLEX

+	$850	1 Bedroom Apartment Rent
+	1,595	2 Bedroom Apartment Rent
-	$1,100	PITI
-	$100	Utilities: Water, Electric, Trash
	$1,245	Net Monthly Profit

FIRST TRIPLEX

+	$1,350	Apartment 1 Rent
+	$950	Apartment 2 Rent
+	$950	Apartment 3 Rent
-	$1,388	PITI
-	$90	Utilities: Water, Electric
	$1,772	Net monthly Profit

SECOND TRIPLEX

+	$825	Apartment 3 Rent
+	$1095	Apartment 2 Rent
+	$1095	Apartment 1 Rent
+	$495	Garage Rent
-	$1,777	PITI
-	$110	Utilities: Water, Electric
	$1,623	Net monthly Profit

SECOND DUPLEX

- \+ $850 Apartment 1 Rent
- \+ $950 Apartment 2 Rent
- \+ $290 Garage Rent
- \- $1,087 PITI
- \- $100 Utilities: Water, Electric, Trash

$1,003 Net monthly Profit

THIRD TRIPLEX

- \+ $850 Apartment 1 Rent
- \+ $925 Apartment 2 Rent
- \+ $550 Apartment 3 Rent
- \- $1,150 Projected Mortgage
- \- $375 Taxes
- \- $100 Insurance
- \- $70 Water
- \- $20 Trash

$610 Net monthly Profit

Our financial picture looked like this:

- \+ $2,558 my monthly take-home pay
- \+ $4,790 net profits on duplex, triplex, triplex with garage
- \+ $1,003 net profits on new duplex with garage
- \+ $610 net profits on newest triplex
- \- $1,581 housing costs for our home
- \- $165 loss on condo carrying costs
- \- $300 loss on truck payment
- \- $0 loss on minivan payment

$6,915 monthly budget

My total Net Monthly Profits were $6,403, not counting my teaching salary. My total monthly housing costs were $1,581, and my truck payment was $300, which left me with a remaining lifestyle budget of $4,207 if I quit my job. Since my family could already live pretty comfortably on a budget of $3,500/month, I considered us to be "financially free," and I made the fated call to arrange my "I quit" meeting with my principal which I related in the introduction. It took seven years and one month from the day my principal "squandered" my hundred hours to retire.

LESSON 31:
DON'T "CIRCLE THE WAGONS"

In the nineteenth century, many Americans traveled westward as the relatively new nation expanded to occupy the continent. Many of these pioneers traveled in wagon trains, or long lines of wagons filled with people, heading west together toward California or Oregon. Inevitably, they began running into the native tribes who already lived on the prairies and plains— and not all of these tribes were friendly. Wagon trains got attacked and people were killed. The pioneers learned that when there was a threat of attack, they could turn their line of wagons into a circle of wagons, which provided a much better defensive position where they could shoot at the natives and protect their own young and weak. This maneuver, "circling the wagons," has become an idiom that means taking up a defensive position in any endeavor.

While I understand the advantages of the formation, there's one problem with it: when you circle the wagons, you are no longer heading west. Pioneers hunkered down behind their circled wagons, watching for natives, aren't marching onward. Permanently circled wagons never make it to California.

During my journey toward financial freedom, I was tempted many times to "circle the wagons." When we were living in our first duplex, I remember thinking to myself *this is good enough. I have a decent job and my family is provided for. I don't want to risk buying the triplex next door. It will be a lot of work, and I don't know what I'm doing. I could fail and put my family in the poorhouse.* During the summer before buying this last triplex, I had similar thoughts. *I've already been very successful, and I'm making more money from real estate than I am at my job. Most people aren't lucky enough to get to this position. I'll just relax and sit tight—I've already risked enough.*

Thankfully, my Realtor's auto-email doesn't know when to quit. I kept looking at new listings, and I kept analyzing them (I was at a point where I could tell very quickly what a good deal looked like), even though I wasn't certain I wanted to continue acquiring real estate. I'm so happy that I continued "plodding toward California." That last triplex pushed my income over the line I needed in order to retire from teaching. Today, that same building nets me around $2,000 per month in income.

All aspiring real estate investors have an existing comfort zone. It consists of what they have already been doing. The routines, habits, job, friends, income, and assumptions we are comfortable with right now will not produce the future that we truly desire. I'm not advocating recklessness—I'm just saying that once you've set your sights on a noble and worthy goal, you're going to need to pursue it with dogged persistence. The alternative is to get discouraged and begin telling yourself "Nebraska is a fine place to live" (no offense if you're from there) and ceasing your "westward journey," never making it to California.

LESSON 32:
ANSWERS ARE BETTER THAN GUESSES

Retiring from a teaching job isn't easy. Yes, you're leaving a steady job with decent benefits and summers off—which is a hard thing to walk away from. Yes, the dominant fear in the mind of a father with a wife and four daughters is they won't be able to afford health insurance. But I'm not referring to those obstacles to retirement. I mean the actual nuts and bolts of following through with it—the PSERS paperwork, the pension money decisions, the conversations with human resources, and my principal. These actual steps are intimidating! I suspect some teachers actually continue teaching (maybe for years) simply because they are intimidated by the steps involved in actually retiring!!

My district held "Retirement Information Nights" at different points during each school year, attended by teachers in their late fifties and early sixties, trying to figure out how much pension income they would be able to count on and how social security and 403b savings plans factored into their retirement timing. The speaker would warn them of proper procedures and possible pitfalls and hand out necessary forms for those teachers who were approaching their last year. I honestly think there are teachers who continued teaching an extra year simply because they missed this meeting!

When I called PSERS, I had no clue whether or not I would be retiring in the fall. But I had already learned to be an action-taker who deals in the currency of answers instead of guesses. Before calling, I guessed that they might think I was weird for retiring at age thirty-five. I guessed that I would have to pay a tax penalty if I wanted to withdraw my cumulative pension contributions (I didn't; I rolled it tax-free into an independent retirement account). I guessed that I'd sound like an idiot because I didn't attend any of the retirement meetings my district had hosted.

None of these things happened. Instead, I reached someone who talked me through the entire process and then sent me the applicable forms. Over the course of two phone calls, I learned exactly how much my bi-weekly paycheck contributions totaled after ten years (plus interest), the amount of my monthly expected pension payments, and how the two numbers affected each other, depending on the amount of my withdrawal. I entered the summer with a clear picture of what my financial picture could look like if I was to find another decent rental property and retire from teaching. Then I found the property—so I retired!

In every step of becoming a real estate investor, you will be tempted to refrain from action because you're operating on the basis of a guess. Go . . . find . . . out!!! It's almost always free or cheap to get the answer you need in order to act. Ask that neighbor with a triplex if he's willing to sell. Call that Realtor and get on an auto-email. Take the steps that turn your guesses into answers. Don't close the door of opportunity without looking through it first—you never know what will be on the other side. And don't operate on the basis of guesses—answers are far better.

LESSON 33:
BELOW-MARKET RENTS ARE A GOOD THING

———

When you have the opportunity to buy a property with below-market rents, do it! Some investors falsely think that low rents are a detriment to the property. Sure, it will mean low revenues for a short time after you purchase, but once you raise the rents at lease renewal or when renting to a new tenant, your income stream will increase. This means that in totality, you will have bought for a low price and yet still eventually received good income. And raising rents to a reasonable level involves no renovation, no repair, and not much work. You simply have to alert the tenants from the beginning that you intend to bring rents to market levels.

In my case, this triplex had rents at $850, $925, and $500. All of these rents were lower than what they should have been, even though the apartments were not in good shape. In one calendar year, I raised the rents to $900, $975, and $650. The only "renovation" I made to the building was to separate the heat. So you could argue that after buying the property, with only the investment of a few minutes re-writing leases, I added $250 in monthly profits. That, combined with the divided heat, brought my monthly cash flow up to $810. In the four years since buying it, I've completely renovated each of the units, one at a time. Now, rents are $1,150, $1,495, and $999—which means my monthly profits are $1,929. It's one of my highest grossing properties, and I would have walked away from it if I'd been turned off by the low rents in place when I purchased.

LESSON 34:
NEGOTIATE REPAIRS INTO PURCHASE PRICE

———

When I got a property inspection on this triplex, the inspector told me that the roof was in poor shape and a significant portion of it needed to be replaced. I quickly called a local roofer and got an estimate on the repairs. When I presented the extra cost to the sellers, they really couldn't argue it—I had done the leg work of quantifying a problem with their property.

I did it quickly so I could respond to the inspections within the contractual deadline for giving them an answer. It meant that I was beginning my ownership of the property with a new roof, and it diminished the need to budget for that type of repair in the future. Make sure to do the same thing: if your inspector finds something that is materially wrong with the property, ask for a discount or a seller credit at closing so that you can make the repair and put your mind at ease. But don't do this with things that are too small or the seller might get fed up and tell you to take a hike.

NOT SO FAST, MISTER!

'd love to tell you that the day after I retired, the shackles fell from my wrists, the scales fell from my eyes, and I became a clear-sighted, free man. After all, my newly acquired income stream pushed me over the level of a comfortable monthly income margin. But I had forgotten one small piece, and it nearly ruined everything!!!

I had acquired the most recent triplex using $188,000 in borrowed cash from my father-in-law. Basically, it was the same money I had borrowed from him multiple times—and he and I both believed I would easily be able to replace it the way I had before. All I needed to do was approach the bank I had used in the past and tell them I wanted to refinance the property.

I started the mortgage application process the day I closed on the triplex. Since the loan officer at the bank I used already had all of my information, my previous tax returns, and the relevant info on my other properties, I really just needed to send him a copy of the new deed, the new leases, and the new desired loan amount. I sent these items via email and waited for his response.

In the first week of September 2015, he asked me if I could drop off a copy of the HUD-1 from the purchase of the triplex (this document is basically the "receipt" listing all of the credits and debits from a sale). I agreed, and I hand-delivered the copy to his office at 10:00 a.m. the next morning. He wasn't there, so I left it with his admin, who I knew from previous visits.

"Thank you," she said. "Are you on a lunch break or something? Who's watching your classroom?"

"Oh—I don't have a classroom anymore. I retired last month."

"Really? How could you retire? How old are you?"

"I'm thirty-five. I'll probably take a few substitute teacher days or something, but I'm done with classroom teaching."

I smiled, wished her a happy day, and walked out of the bank without giving the conversation a second thought. The next day, I got a phone call from the loan officer at the bank.

"What were you thinking? Coming in here and bragging about quitting your job? That didn't go over so well with my loan committee. The reason we've been comfortable loaning you money is you've had a steady job with a regular salary to help smooth out any hiccups along the way. Without your job, you are no longer as attractive of a loan candidate."

My stomach almost came out of my throat. I literally forced back tears while on the phone with him. "But . . . these new rents, plus the rents from the places I already have, more than make up for my lost salary. And I'm in a better position now to take care of my places and monitor tenants and collect rents and everything else."

"Well, I'll explain that to my loan committee," he replied. "But I don't know how far it will go. I could have maybe eked the loan through if you hadn't blabbed in the office about retiring. "

I waited a week and didn't hear anything back from him. I called and left a message every other day after that, and still didn't hear anything for another week. I was panicked. When I finally got in touch with him, he told me that his loan committee wasn't meeting again for another week or so and that he would get back in touch with me then. He never did, which is why I'm glad I didn't wait for his sorry butt.

Instead, I told myself, "You will figure this out—don't panic!" First of all, my father-in-law didn't need the money back immediately. Since it was coming from a LOC and I was willing to cover the interest payments while the money was borrowed, it didn't hurt him. Still, I wanted to give him back the money as soon as I possibly could.

I also started taking action. Since any bank would probably want to see some type of earned income, I signed up to be a substitute teacher in my school district—a process which was actually WAY harder than it should have been for someone with a master's degree and ten years of teaching experience. They paid $90/day to subs, and there were opportunities to substitute teach every single school day. If necessary, this meant I could earn an income of around $1,800 per month as a sub. On top of that, I had elected to begin receiving my monthly pension immediately upon retirement. This meant I was entitled to less than if I had waited until age sixty, but I figured it was worthwhile to have the money in hand now. Since the payment amount is $150/month, which brought my potential "salary" to $1,950, it was a good choice.

I also began calling some of the other local banks near me to ask if they would extend the same mortgage products that the previous bank had. I made sure not to tell them that I was "retired" but that I had a position as a substitute teacher for as many days per month as I needed, up to about $1,800. After four or five conversations with loan officers at other banks, I found one who could extend a mortgage to me with roughly the same terms I needed. The only potential issue was that they would be contracting with an appraiser from outside the area. But I couldn't be too choosy, so I plowed ahead.

I paid $400 out of pocket to the bank for the appraisal fee and met the appraiser at the property, then walked him through each of the units. I explained that I had replaced a good portion of the roof and that I had divided the heat—both of which I felt added value to the property.

"Well, maybe," he said. "It all depends on what comparable triplexes in the area have been selling for." As it turned out, a triplex had just sold a few weeks earlier on the other side of town (a much less desirable part of town) for $160,000.

When the appraisal report came back, it was not for as much as I had wanted. "$205,000?" I shouted when I opened the email from my loan officer. I showed Kelly.

"What does that mean for us?" she asked.

"It means I can't pay your dad back all of the money that I borrowed," I answered. The bank will only lend us 80 percent of the appraisal value—which is $164,000. I owe your dad $188,000."

"Talk to him and see if you can work out a payment plan. He knows, by this point, that you're good for it." So that's what I ended up doing—we settled with the bank on a mortgage for $164,000 and my father-in-law kept a $22,000 line of credit, which I paid him for each month. Since he was getting a better rate on this LOC than I was getting with my new mortgage, it actually ended up being cheaper to finance it in such a way.

LESSON 35:
DON'T CELEBRATE (OR RETIRE!) TOO EARLY

I root for the Philadelphia Eagles football team. A few years ago, a wide receiver named DeSean Jackson played for them. He was lightning fast with hands like glue, and he loved to showboat and celebrate. In a game against their division rivals, the Dallas Cowboys, DeSean Jackson faked out his defensive back, streaked past the safety, and caught a sixty-one-yard pass. As he was crossing the goal line, Jackson leisurely tossed the ball aside and began a celebration dance in the end zone.

Upon instant replay review, however, the camera clearly showed that Jackson had actually dropped the ball before he crossed the goal line. The touchdown was reversed and the points were taken off the scoreboard! The play is commonly shown on countdowns of "NFL's most embarrassing moments" and is used to drive home the lesson: never celebrate too early.

I should not have quit my job when I did! Obviously, it almost tanked my chances of finding financing for my last acquisition. I desperately wanted to walk away before the school year began, but I didn't need to. Even though I was already making far more in real estate than I was making from my teaching salary, I definitely underestimated how much the bank would care about my keeping this salary. Although it wasn't fair for the loan officer to label what I did as "bragging" (I just told his admin the truth!), it obviously would have been wiser to have been more discreet.

If you're an aspiring real estate investor, don't quit your job to pursue real estate. You may need that job to grow your real estate holdings. And, like me, you may end up needing that job for far longer than you expect. I think it is a noble goal to build assets that eventually replace your income, freeing you up to quit your day job. But doing so before being 100 percent prepared may have dire consequences. If you end up in a circumstance similar to mine, remain employed until your last refinance is completed, then retire.

LESSON 36:
DON'T FREEZE THE MONEY

Up to this point, I had been fairly fortunate with regard to returning borrowed money to my father-in-law. My renovations had increased the value of my properties so the new mortgage gave me enough money to pay back this personal debt. But in this latest triplex, I got hung up on a comp appraisal. Even though I had divided the heat—which made my property more profitable and thus more valuable—the appraiser had to establish the value of my property by finding something that had sold recently and was fairly similar to mine. He picked a craphole property as a comp, so his overall appraisal was low.

In fairness, the correct way to determine the market value for anything is to find what people are willing to pay for similar items. In real estate, the way to answer this question is to find out what people recently paid for a reasonably similar property.

In my case, the most recent sale for a triplex in Bethlehem wasn't very high, and since the appraiser's estimation of value has to start somewhere, it meant my triplex wasn't valued as highly as I had hoped—which meant I couldn't get a new mortgage amount sufficient to fully repay my father-in-law. I was very lucky that he didn't mind, and that he allowed us to make payments on the outstanding balance we owed him until we were able to pay it off fully.

Make sure to have a backup plan if a property does not appraise as high as you need it to. In many cases, you can appeal the appraisal and provide reasons you believe the value is higher to the appraiser. Sometimes they will revise their appraisal report and send a new value to the bank, which means you will have access to a higher loan.

VACUUMING MY TRUCK

After retiring from teaching, acquiring health insurance, and squaring away all of the financing on my last property, I still wasn't completely financially comfortable. Our "lifestyle budget" of $4,207 per month (after paying for our housing and my truck) meant we could save money at a decent rate and begin to accumulate a reserve fund for the apartments, in case any major expenses arose.

But I wanted to optimize as much as possible. I began to realize that the $300/month Toyota Tundra I "needed" during the pinnacle of my renovations wasn't quite as necessary anymore. On most days, it was a 5,000-pound vehicle carrying around a 200-pound man—not the most financially efficient solution to my commuting needs. I certainly felt like a "man's man" driving around in a truck—but the gas costs, higher insurance costs, and higher registration fees meant that my vanity was expensive! I resolved to sell the truck and rid myself of the excessive costs.

There was one problem. Although I had sold vehicles in the past, I'd always managed to sell a vehicle that I owned outright. My truck, however, still had a $9,800 loan.

In Pennsylvania, the state holds on to the title for a car or truck until the loan is paid off. Once this happens, the bank holding the loan instructs the state to send the "clear" title to the owner.

But in my case, in order for me to sell the truck to a buyer, I would need to have the title in hand when arriving at the notary to transfer title, at which point the buyer would give me their money. Yet if I didn't have the money before going to the notary, I would have no way to pay off the loan ahead of time, which meant I wouldn't have the title in hand. In other words, it was a classic catch-22.

I let this predicament freeze me for months, making payments on the loan and paying for a gas-guzzling, V8-engine, truck-as-commuter-vehicle. I didn't know how to solve the issue, and I figured I'd have to wait a few years until I had paid the truck off in small monthly payments. I had spent a good bit of cash separating the heat on the most recent triplex acquisition and hadn't been able to accumulate enough to fully pay off the truck.

But in November of 2015, I was sitting at my desk (no more day job!) and checking my bank accounts online. I saw my $300 auto-draft payment for my truck deducted from my accounts, and I mentally committed myself to get free from the payment. "I still do not know how I am going to sell a truck when it has a loan on it, but this shouldn't stop me from at least vacuuming out my truck," I thought. I had a Shop-Vac in the garage, so I took it outside and vacuumed my truck that same day.

The next day, I thought, "I still don't know how to sell a truck with a loan on it, but I do know how to wash my truck." So I did. I hooked up the hose and washed the truck. These first two steps cost nothing.

The following day, I thought, "I don't know how to sell a truck with a loan on it, but I can get my wife to take pictures of the truck—and that's still free!" So that's exactly what we did. Later that day, we created a Craigslist ad for the truck at $11,000 and published it online.

Within a few days, I started to get calls from interested buyers. I was terrified! I had NO clue what to tell these people if they actually wanted to buy my truck! But I proceeded to schedule test-drives with interested shoppers anyway, deciding that I would wait until somebody actually wanted to buy my truck before even attempting to figure out what to do afterward. After all, I didn't know how to sell a truck with a loan on it, but I DID know how to give test-drives.

A week and a half later, a middle-aged gentleman contacted me and asked if we could do a test-drive. I agreed. He pulled up outside in a newer Toyota Tundra. When I came outside, he said to me, "These have always been great trucks for me. My son is in the market for one, but he lives an hour away. I agreed to do his test driving for him."

I gave him the keys and hopped into the passenger seat. We drove it around the block, then out to the 45 mph road a few blocks over. He brought it up to speed and then turned around in a parking lot a mile down the road. We drove in reverse, then he switched on the four-wheel-drive, honked the horn, checked all the headlights, locked it with the remote key, looked at the tires, and more.

"I'll take it," he said. "$11,000 is a decent price."

At this point, I was out of answers. I couldn't lie to the guy, so I told him the truth.

"I actually have a loan on this truck—so I'm not in possession of the title. If you're serious, you will probably have to pay me the money so I can pay off the loan. Then we can wait for the title to arrive in the mail and just go to the notary as soon as I have it."

"I'm not going to do that," he said (this is exactly what a smart person would say). "But here's what I will do—I'll give you a $500 deposit today to hold the truck and take down your ad. This assures me you won't sell it to anybody else and it assures you I won't back out. Do whatever you can to get hold of the rest of the money—borrow from family or your 401k or something—and pay off the loan. When you get the title in the mail, I will come back and give you the rest of the money, and we'll go to the notary and transfer the title."

"Hmmm. I can probably do that. Should we sign a contract or something in the meantime?"

"I think that's a good idea. You write me a receipt for the $500 deposit and a bill of sale for the remaining amount. We'll meet and sign when you have the title."

That's exactly what we did. I printed out the bill of sale and receipt on my computer and brought it outside for him to sign. He gave me the $500 and then left.

I had $500 in cash but needed to come up with another $9,300 to pay off the loan. After a conversation with my wife where we agreed to put everything on credit cards for the next week and a half, I used all of our cash in the bank plus all of my escrow totals that I was saving toward real estate taxes and insurance premium payments for our rental properties. The banks I held mortgages with allowed me to self-escrow these funds, so I had easy (and legal) access to them.

Although the maneuver brought us dangerously close to $0 in liquid funds, I put all of the money into one account and then sent a check for the outstanding balance to the bank holding my auto loan. Five days later, the title arrived in the mail and I immediately called the buyer.

We ended up doing exactly as we had planned. I met him at the notary and signed the title over to him. He gave me an envelope full of cash, which I carefully counted. $11,000, all there. We shook hands and he drove the truck away (to pick up his son, so they could both come back and retrieve his newer truck from the notary parking lot).

I deposited the money in my bank, replaced all of the amounts I had withdrawn from my escrow accounts, and had $1,200 remaining to put toward another, cheaper car.

Two weeks later (after collecting rents) I saw a Mazda 3 hatchback for sale for $2,000. I talked the seller down to $1,800 and bought it. Five weeks later, I sold the Mazda for $3,000, which I then used to buy a Honda CR-V with 106,000 miles on it.

To this day, the Honda CR-V is still the best machine I have ever owned and it is still the car I drive. I've never had a loan on it, it gets excellent gas mileage, it has All-Wheel Drive, and it even has a lift-glass in the tailgate which allows me to carry ten-foot-long 2x4s when necessary.

This endeavor reduced my monthly costs by over $300 as compared to when I owned the Tundra (when factoring in things like insurance, registration, and gas costs). However, all of my transportation needs were still met and the vehicle has been reliable and has allowed me to handle landlording responsibilities easily.

If I had simply sat still when I concluded that I don't know how to sell a truck with a loan on it, I never would have gotten out from under the $300/month loan.

I find that most people, when faced with a problem like this, resign themselves to the status quo. They can't see what step 5 is going to look like, so they don't bother taking step 1–step 4. But most of the time, you don't get to see step 5 until you're standing on step 4. The crowning irony is that steps 1–4 are often free, just like the steps involved in selling my truck. Sure, I had to take a risky step by temporarily spending all of my free cash to pay off the loan—but I did that with the knowledge that a buyer was ready and waiting.

On the day I went outside to vacuum my truck, I certainly wasn't ready to empty all of my escrow accounts to help pay off the loan—I hadn't even known it was going to come to that. But paying off the loan would have been impossible without first vacuuming the truck.

As I look back on my real estate investing career, this transaction serves as a tidy parable for the mindset that has made me successful. I had no clue what I was doing when I got started. In fact, my investing career started in the negative.

Yet mostly out of sheer panic and economic necessity, my wife and I were forced to begin attempting things and making small, scary little decisions that have added up to decent successes. Almost none of the steps involved have been more difficult than vacuuming my truck. I've just accumulated thousands of similarly simple steps at this point, which impress even me when I view their net effect.

As I write this paragraph, my home is under contract. My wife and I listed it for sale by owner and within a week had an offer above listing price. If we manage to make it through settlement, it will have been a fairly profitable investment for us while also housing our family for the last six years. But five months ago, I employed the "vacuum the truck" mentality.

On a perfectly sunny day, when our deck, patio, and in-ground pool were spotless, I said, "Kelly—get your camera out and take showing pictures of the pool, yard, patio, and deck. Make sure to save them in a file on our desktop."

Weeks later, on a day when the renovated kitchen was spotless and the afternoon light was "just right" I said, "Kelly—this time of day is perfect for taking 'showing' pics of our kitchen, don't you think?" She agreed, and we saved a few more on the computer desktop file.

A week and a half ago, we saw a house that really has the potential to be a "forever house" for our family. We immediately put in an offer. Without breaking a sweat, as soon as our offer was accepted, my wife created a Zillow ad for our current home. Since we had all of the most beautiful pictures of our house already saved, she just had to upload them and then input the description and the data. It took about forty-five minutes because she wanted it to be perfect. Now, a week later, our home is under contract because we "vacuumed the truck."

If you are a normal person, there is something in your life right now that could amount to "vacuuming the truck." Sit down and just think for five minutes about what needs to change or improve in your life or economic condition. Start writing down things you want to alter. If you own a gas-guzzling truck you don't need, start by doing exactly what I did. Or use the mantra "vacuum the truck" symbolically as you attack other parts of your life. The steps you take might work, or they might not. But you'll never sell your truck unless you take the time to vacuum it first.

ACKNOWLEDGMENTS

Thank you to my wife, Kelly, for being my partner in life and in business.

Thank you to my parents, Dan and Kathy Stewart, for giving me a cheater's edge in life.

Thank you to my in-laws, Dave and Linda Dyson, for believing in me and lending seed capital and helping us paint and landscape.

Thank you to Tony Stancato for giving me your time and for going to bat for me at a critical juncture in my journey.

Thank you to Rock Thomas, Matt Eng, Joe Perkins, Linzee & Steve Ciprani and all of M1 for providing a community for high achievers.

Thank you to Matthew Johnson (Contracting) for being the most honest and hardworking GC around.

Thank you to my daughters, for following Daddy around when he needed to go to the hardware store or a million other errands.

Thank you to Ryan Feauve, for being a jack of all trades.

Thank you to Bigger Pockets, for empowering people like me to get connected and informed.

Thank you to Jon Bryan, Jason Daily, Stu Keogh, Brian Mason, Peter Snedeker, and Paul Steinweg for being brothers and friends who all excel.

Thank you to Jaiden, for being a sounding board and an eager student.

Thank you to Peter Kurtz, for being a friend and a fellow laborer toward truly enduring investments.

Thanks to Tony Steck, unbelievably gifted cover designer, book formatter, and friend.

ABOUT THE AUTHOR

Bryce Stewart lives and invests in Bethlehem, PA with his beautiful wife and four daughters. A chance encounter at age twenty three demonstrated to him that wealth can be generated from opportunities besides a high paying job. This experience planted a seed in his mind that germinated and fully blossomed as Bryce and his wife began "House Hacking" their way to financial freedom, using live-in rental properties to create a cash flowing portfolio that eventually allowed Bryce and his wife to retire from their full time jobs.

CAN YOU HELP?

THANK YOU FOR READING MY BOOK!

I really appreciate all of your feedback,
and I love hearing what you have to say.

I need your input to make the next version of
this book and my future books better.

Please leave me an honest review on Amazon
letting me know what you thought of the book.

Thanks so much!

Bryce Stewart

Made in the USA
Middletown, DE
29 December 2020